'*Pictures of God* combines a profound th
and God's purpose in the world with
in a complex, diverse and pluralistic tv

'Founded in the Bible and widely
with a wealth of contemporary illustrations, this book offers insignt
and challenge for Christian disciples and leaders in every context.

'Reminding us of the relational nature of God and the dynamic
mission that flows from the Trinity, this demanding and inspired
volume will refocus communities on Christ Jesus. Jesus' desire to draw
all people to Himself in a new identity of love and service will flourish
as we seek to put the principles of *Pictures of God* in to practice.'
The Rt Rev David Urquhart (Bishop of Birmingham)

'For those used to a logo-centric style of doing theology, *Pictures of God:
Shaping Missional Church Life* may come as a surprise. Launching from
the certainties of the word through to the "impressionism" of images
may seem to jettison unchangeable securities, but as Andy Hardy's
survey shows, this is precisely what Scripture itself does. Fresh images
are themselves demanded by new forms of Christian community and
experience, both in the first century and today. The emerging church
context of this book calls for integrated contextual theology of this kind.
It shows how the movement from practical engagement to theological
reflection to transformative response and back again actually works. In
opening up divided communities to the mission of God, Hardy shows
how God's triune nature may be newly comprehended in multicultural
terms.'
*Dr John Moxon, Senior Lecturer in Ministerial Theology, University of
Roehampton, London*

'This is a rare but vitally important text that combines passion for
mission, academic rigour, and an embracing overview of key issues in
contextual contemporary ministry. Having worked with Andy over a
number of years in academic teaching, shared writing and local
ministry engagement, I know this book is a genuine expression of his
own heart.

'The kind of leadership we need today is from those who will take
risks, who will pioneer and learn to live and lead outside the
comfortable frameworks to envision and enable something new. It is

my belief that this work is an important tool that can aid in this discovery and release of new kinds of leadership that will encourage dreaming of the kingdom to come in our day. The prophetic insight that he brings should enable all those who read and work with this volume to discover the *missio Trinitatis* as a living and empowering presence to enable authentic missional leadership and ministry in the twenthy-first century.'

Dan Yarnell, National Coordinator, the Fellowship of Churches of Christ in Great Britain and Ireland

'*Pictures of God: Shaping Missional Church Life* is a rich gift to those of us who are intentionally seeking to enflesh Christian communities in cities, suburbs and villages. Moving between biblical, systematic, cultural and visual disciplines Andy Hardy opens important vistas for teachers, practitioners and students. This rich resource weaves together vital ingredients while always offering space for application in local and specific contexts, and that enables the reader sight of the creative work of the Holy Spirit. This is a fine example of theological reflection at its best and now sits on our essential reading list for those we teach and research with at Stirling.'

Dr Andrew Menzies, Principal, Stirling Theological College – University of Divinity, Australia

'In the book Andy unpacks his central idea: that the Trinity, as a multicultural missional family, should be a model of mission that welcomes all peoples, in our multicultural societies, to be a part of and play their part in God's family, made up of all peoples. If you want to find out how Andy's thesis relates to you, you need to read his fascinating book yourself.'

Dave Andrews community worker, activist and author of A Divine Society: The Trinity, Community and Society

'People are moving as migrants around the world as never before. The arrival of so many from other continents to the shores of western lands produces fascinating challenges and opportunities. Andrew Hardy's motif of "pictures" of God provides a fascinating canvas for seeing afresh the opportunities before us.'

Martin Robinson, CEO of ForMission and Principal of ForMission College, Birmingham

Pictures of God

Shaping Missional Church Life

Andrew R. Hardy

instant
apOstle

First published in Great Britain by Instant Apostle, 2016.

Instant Apostle
The Barn
1 Watford House Lane
Watford
Herts
WD17 1BJ

The views and opinions expressed in this work are those of the author and do not necessarily reflect the views and opinions of the publisher.

British Library Cataloguing-in-Publication Data

A catalogue record for this book is available from the British Library

This book and all other Instant Apostle books are available from Instant Apostle:

Website: www.instantapostle.com

E-mail: info@instantapostle.com

ISBN 978-1-909728-40-0

Printed in Great Britain

Instant Apostle is a way of getting ideas flowing, between followers of Jesus, and between those who would like to know more about His kingdom.

It's not just about books and it's not about a one-way information flow. It's about building a community where ideas are exchanged. Ideas will be expressed at an appropriate length. Some will take the form of books. But in many cases ideas can be expressed more briefly than in a book. Short books, or pamphlets, will be an important part of what we provide. As with pamphlets of old, these are likely to be opinionated, and produced quickly so that the community can discuss them.

Well-known authors are welcome, but we also welcome new writers. We are looking for prophetic voices, authentic and original ideas, produced at any length; quick and relevant, insightful and opinionated. And as the name implies, these will be released very quickly, either as Kindle books or printed texts or both.

Join the community. Get reading, get writing and get discussing!

Dedication

I dedicate this book to all of my brothers and sisters in Christ in the family of God. To my mother Sylvia, my Father Jack and my brother Alan. To Jenny, Lizzy and Tim all of who have taught me how to value family and love being part of their lives.

Also with many thanks to my dear friend Dan Yarnell, who has been so much a part of reflecting on the big themes I explore in this book over the 11 years we have known each other. We enjoy opportunities to reflect, as well as to write together. I look forward to many more chances to do this.

And thanks to students who have engaged on courses I have taught, as they have helped me to think through how to communicate my ideas in fresh ways, based on their challenging questions and many helpful reflections. We come to know things better when we share our hearts, thoughts and feelings in the context of community.

Andrew R. Hardy, October 2015

Contents

Note to the reader

This book is a companion to *Forming Multicultural Partnerships: Church Planting in a Divided Society*, which was written by my colleague Dan Yarnell and me. That first volume contains practical applications which are needed to engage in multicultural mission in the West. I would suggest that it is worth reading that book alongside this one in order to obtain maximum benefit from both.

Andrew R. Hardy, July 2015

Introduction

This book uses the phrase 'pictures of God' in a particular sense. Human language first emerged in the form of pictographs around 5,000 years ago. We see this in the ancient Egyptian hieroglyphs that still adorn ritual sites in Egypt today. We also see examples of hieroglyphs on many artefacts in places like the British Museum.

The most profound use of language in its earliest incarnations sought to picture what humans thought God might look like. Literal pictorial representations of the gods were drawn or made into images. Indeed, the way people in the Ancient Near East communicated in signs and symbols, about their gods, suggests that language began with pictures which represented words.

In the Hebrew Scriptures, God is not portrayed in images but rather in words and stories. These word pictures of God sought to describe qualities of Yahweh, such as His love and faithfulness. These word pictures were drawn in order to reveal Yahweh's nature and character to His people, and were constructed through the narratives of God's dealings with His people. Hence when I talk about churches having a picture of God, I especially mean narrative-based identities defined in word descriptions. When the Son of God became a living, breathing human being, God was translated into a real person wanting real relationships with real people. The Son of God began to restore the image of God in humankind through His perfect life to be conveyed to them by the presence of His Spirit.

The picture of God we most relate to is that of Christ: His life, teachings, death, resurrection, ascension and the coming of His Spirit into our hearts. Christ's face is said to mystically shine in our hearts in 2 Corinthians 4:1-6. In other words, our picture of God is spiritually brought to life by the indwelling Christ. The indwelling

Christ shines through our life stories and through the corporate personas of our Christian communities, as His modern-day disciples partake in Christ's image.

People like to picture what God is like through the stories they tell each other about Him. In this book, I suggest that our Christian communities create word pictures and stories of God. Stories have a wonderful capacity to enable us to picture ourselves in them. It is not enough to say that 'God is love': we need to have examples and experiences related to us to help us bring our own pictures of God to life.

My thesis in this book is that people often join our churches because they like the picture of God that is portrayed through the people they relate to. The stories about God that we convey to faith-seekers are often based on our own stories which demonstrate how God has acted in our lives. In a real sense, the best picture of God to communicate to others is the kind that comes from our own experiences and those of others. People are missionally impacted by the pictures of God upon which we base our life stories. We make decisions to become part of a faith community based on our impression of the picture of God that shapes its beliefs and practices.

In the chapters which follow we will unpack how important our corporate pictures of God are to the formation of our self-identity and the identity of our corporate persona, which in turn project the identity of our faith community to others. We will also consider how important they are to conveying our faith to faith-seekers.

In part one we will consider how Christian identity is formed from a psychological perspective, through the gospels and as an integral part of our human design, as we consider what it means to be made in the image of God. If we accept that we bear the image of God's character in Christ, this enables us to construct our social identities as Christian missional communities.

In part two we will consider the biblical foundations of the picture of God as missionary. God in Christ sent the Son of God to redeem the world. Moreover, Christ sends believers to engage in His continuing mission. The picture of Christ the missionary informs His followers' mission to engage in His continuing work to reconcile people to God's family. The Trinity's mission is to reconcile all peoples and cultures into God's cosmic new community.

In part three we explore the idea that the Trinity family is based on God's mission, through which God sends His people out in the power of the Spirit of Jesus to help others to form a meaningful relationship with God. When I use the term 'Trinity family', I do so as a metaphor for what it means to be sons and daughters of God. It is important to understand that the picture of God the missionary informs my metaphor of the Trinity having a multicultural mission as well. The Trinity as our Father, Mother, Brother and Sister creates a view of the God who welcomes all peoples, nations and cultures into His cosmic family. This is the work of the Multicultural Trinity (MT). Obviously the use of the metaphor MT is not the same as using it literally to define who God the Trinity is in nature and substance. This would represent a gross theological error that would equate Godself with a human category of understanding which is not the same as a divine category, which is revealed to the church as an absolute statement about the nature of God.

Part four considers how to help our Christian communities to operate out of a place of deep fellowship with the living presence of the Holy Spirit who exists in the hearts of all believers. Deep spiritual connection needs to be available to God's people through their spiritual practices. God is active and alive in our communities. Our experience of communion with God brings our pictures of God alive, and we can experience His intimate love for ourselves.

In the final part we will consider how we can help our churches to construct their identities more intelligently by helping them to become more aware of what their picture/s of God is/are.

May God bless you as you read this book.

Part 1

How pictures of God are formed

Chapter 1
Social identity and a Christian group's picture of God

Upon what picture of God does your church base its identity? This question is a useful starting point for this chapter. There is power in identity. People gather around shared identities in order to bring meaning and purpose to their lives. We gather in the groups to which we belong, based on a common social identity. The power of social group identity is its ability to join people together to fulfil similar goals. Our pictures of God help to frame the way we think about His purposes for our communities and their part in participation in *missio Dei* ('God's mission').

In this book we will consider how a group's picture of what God is like directly impacts the identity of the people who belong to that group. Our social identities are based on how we picture ourselves as part of a group. The sociologists Tajfel and Turner developed social identity theory[1] which, according to the pastoral psychologist Collicutt,

> holds that people form group affiliations because these provide them with a source of both personal identity and self-esteem. The groups we belong to tell us something about who we are, and we may feel that we have some kudos from being part of the group.[2]

---

[1] H. Tajfel and J. C. Turner, 'An integrative theory of intergroup conflict', in W. G. Austin and S. Worchel (eds.), *The Social Psychology of Intergroup Relations*, Monterey: Brooks Cole (1979), pp. 33-40.

[2] Joanna Collicutt, *The Psychology of Christian Character Formation*, Norwich: SCM Press (2015), p. 163.

Christians who belong to a particular church which is part of a specific denomination will often embrace the norms and values of that church and will draw their identity from them. This is a powerful force which keeps people together and motivates Christian movements to fulfil God's mission in their particular context. A group's identity is formed by the beliefs its members have about God and the practices in which they engage, which inform their behaviours among the people with whom they associate in their daily lives.

Having noted this positive angle to social identity, Collicutt points out a downside of social group identity:

> Social identity is ... not value-free. It plays itself out in ethnocentricism – the preference for all aspects of one's group over others, and behaviour that favours this group over others. As it is important to be able to recognize the members of one's group, identity markers that can effectively differentiate between groups become important. In addition to habits ... these may involve aspects of appearance such as clothing, the assent to certain key beliefs, or forms of speech and language.[3]

The mainline denominations in the UK do not seek to segregate their members from other Christian groups, as was the case in a past age. This is a positive development. We still see it happening among some denominational groups such as Seventh Day Adventists at times, and Evangelical Reformed churches can also tend towards separatism. The ecumenical spirit is now more broadly valued, which means that local churches of different denominations are partnering more regularly. It is still the case, however, that different denominational groups gather around key beliefs and practices by which group members identify themselves. For example, when I meet with Christian leaders from other denominations at conferences, I often find that we discuss what we can learn from our different backgrounds. I may find myself making a supportive

---

[3] Collicutt, *The psychology of Christian Character Formation*, p. 163.

statements to colleagues from other denominations, to the effect, 'I think it is important for us to practise what we believe, and that is something I like about the Fellowship of Churches of Christ.' Responses like these are obviously informed by our own self-narratives, which help us to identify who we are compared to another Christian group.

How we identify who we are to others

What we say about ourselves to people from other groups can lead to the formation of friendships, which can enable us to identify shared common ground. Missiologists term intentional friendships 'incarnational behaviour', which is necessary if we want to form meaningful friendships. Such partnerships are based on issues in which both parties have passion to engage – for example, because of a common desire to give food to needy families in the local community. The rapid rise of foodbanks is a good example of Christian groups gathering around a common theme represented in Christ's ministry. Christ sought to address the immediate needs of people, which in turn formed a bridge for Him to help them consider their eternal destinies. Christ is portrayed in the gospels as the answer to humanity's deepest need, which is the restoration of the image of God in mankind.

Christians of different persuasions can gather around Jesus their Lord, based on their shared identity as those who are being transformed into the likeness of Christ. The Son of God incarnated among humans in order to provide them with a role model upon which to base their identities. All Christians share a common identity because they are all being transformed by the inner Christ into His likeness. It is this inner Christ who motivates how Christians behave as much as the ways their cultures have shaped how they express who they are in a given context. Christians need to be incarnational with each other so that they may provide a picture of Christ as they share together a life based on service to God and others. When we incarnate into each other's worlds, we do so based on shared pictures of Christ the Lord who unites us by His

21

Spirit as the body of Christ. The universal body of Christ transcends national, racial, gender and culture-related barriers that can stop people from relating to each other. We need to form partnerships that transcend these boundaries so that we can offer friendship and support where it is needed within the local community, which is often multicultural and pluralistic.

Pictures of Christ shared in common unite people

Simply stated, the pictures of Christ that we share in common help us to join together as one body of Christ. The body of the universal Christ transcends the ethnocentric limitations that have historically kept Christians apart, living as they have in their own social identity groups. For example, the advent of new migrant Christian groups on our doorsteps provides evidence of how identity is so important to help sustain a faith group. In our multicultural society we see the planting of first- and second-generation migrant churches. To begin with, each of these churches is normally made up of one people group – for example, there are Nigerian churches, Ethiopian churches, or Polish churches.

Differing pictures of God can mean that each of these cultural Christian groups becomes segregated from other groups because the first generation of migrants has a tendency to stick together in order to maintain their cultural identity. Moreover, some migrant churches build their identities around protecting

> **Identity based on good deeds like those of Christ**
>
> New Life Church, Brighton
>
> 'Our vision is a picture of what we "see" ourselves becoming as we grow together, becoming more like Jesus. We can see in God's word [that] we, the church, can be a people so filled with the Light of Christ that He is pleased to lift us up, like a city on a hill that cannot be hidden, shedding light in such a way that people see our good deeds and praise our father in heaven. We see ourselves, under Christ, becoming such a people.'
>
> https://www.newlifebrighton.org.uk/vision-statement.html

their people from being 'corrupted' by the secular West where they now live.

Some of my colleagues have been building intentional relationships with ethnic churches. We are finding that we and they share a passion to help each other to share the gospel in our multicultural society. (When I speak of 'multicultural society' in this volume I include postmodern Western people who gather in smaller subcultural groups, known by sociologists as 'new tribes'. These cultural groups are also part of the fabric of Western pluralistic and multicultural society.)

One picture of God that sustains a monocultural ethnic church's identity can be expressed in terms of God's people living in exile in a foreign land with God the protector sustaining them. It is noteworthy that many African immigrant churches in the West use the Old Testament Scriptures to inform their Christian community of stories that can help them cope with the transition to life in the West. This is probably because many of the Old Testament stories of displacement, exile, nomadic journeying and so on are rich sources of inspiration in which migrants can find help to interpret their own journeys as they seek to establish new lives in the West. Their social identities come out of their own stories of travel to a new land, as well as the stories of how God travelled with His chosen people Israel, in the Tabernacle, as they moved from place to place in their 40 years of wilderness wandering.[4] They need to do this in order to function psychologically well in a strange new culture.

Christian identity that sustains peoples in transition

It is important to recognise that storytelling of human journeys is not uncommon for people in transition from one place to another. We find stories of God's people in transition in the Bible and in church history. For example, when the Pilgrim Fathers left Europe

---

[4] See Numbers 1–10.

to escape persecution in early seventeenth-century Europe, they founded Christian colonies in North America. They took with them their desire to live out their faith with freedom from persecution. Subsequently, as Christian colonies were founded, some of these Christian pioneers became frontiersmen, going on a voyage of discovery to find new territories in North America to settle their families. Their stories were largely informed by a theology of pilgrimage. Part of their missional journey included taking the Christian faith to the Native American Indian peoples. Boundary crossing, with Christ at the side of these brave men, women and children, became an identifying narrative which still informs American patriotism. It is recognisable in their active devotion to the flag which represents the land of the free.

The Pilgrim Fathers believed they were following Christ to a land of new freedoms and opportunities. The picture of Christ as both liberator and peacemaker informed their faith narratives and journeys. Moreover, the American codified Constitution builds its convictions on the separation of the church and the state. In Europe, the state and church joined forces to forbid religious liberty when it went against accepted religious norms, whereas the US Constitution was informed by the theological vision of liberty from oppression, and sought to protect religious freedoms and rights from state-administered persecution. It is true that the Black Civil Rights Movement of the 1950s and 1960s protested against the discrimination of Black people in US society. We cannot forget the story of Martin Luther King Jr and his martyrdom in order to obtain equal rights for Blacks in America. His sacrifice was a direct consequence of his protest, which led to equal civil rights being given to Black people in the end.

King's story – indeed, the Black Civil Rights Movement – was largely constructed around the narrative of the suffering Christ, where King and his supporters followed in the Saviour's footsteps to protest and to seek justice and liberation for Black people. The land of the free needed to be reminded that the ideals of the persecuted Pilgrim Fathers were in fact the same as the ideals of the

Black Civil Rights Movement – the right of their people to live free from discrimination.

The US Constitution was founded upon freedom and non-discrimination and came about directly because of the picture of Christ the peacemaker and liberator. The Civil Rights Movement embraced the same picture as their forebears, who had sought to embed freedom into the new land to which they had been led.

All of what we have considered so far demonstrates that a whole country – indeed, what is generally regarded as the most powerful nation in the world – took its codified constitutional identity from the picture of God the freedom giver. I might add that in order for God's mission to be realised with the unification of all tongues, peoples and nations by the love of God in Christ, it will be important for governments and peoples in our nations and societies to be helped to reconnect with what are often deep Christian convictions that shaped their societies during the time of Christendom. God's kingdom comes on earth as in heaven when groups connect with Christ the Messiah.

A foretaste of the kingdom of God conveyed through the Christian community

The scholar and historian N. T. Wright challenges us to understand that the kingdom of God is not something of the future (only), but that Christ is already King of the kingdom of God of which we are part.[5] This is not to deny that there will be a final tipping point when Christ returns and the kingdom of God is fully manifested in a new world order, governed by God's love. The stories and sayings of Jesus, found in the gospels, show us a picture of Christ building a kingdom community of disciples in the present world. Christ wants us to live out kingdom life in the world we live in today.

It is through our Christian communities that the new society of the kingdom of God is pictured and portrayed to secular peoples.

---

[5] N. T. Wright, *The New Testament and the People of God*, London: SPCK (1992), pp.285-289.

Our Christian communities can frame a new Christlike identity, where unity and diversity cause people to live in harmony with one another. Faith-seekers may also use communities like this as reference points to construct their identities.

The kingdom is in the process of coming. In the Lord's Prayer Jesus taught His disciples to pray, 'Your kingdom come. Your will be done, on earth as it is in heaven.'[6]

God is already king of everything, even though His reign is not yet fully manifest in our societies. As we engage in making disciples of all people in every strata of our multicultural pluralistic society, we need to be praying that our lives model the life of Christ whose love unites all peoples. The kingdom is coming now, although in another sense it is not yet. We must be careful not to project it into the future and leave it there without also praying for its influence to grow in our communities, like the proverbial mustard seed of Jesus' kingdom parable.

If we push the kingdom of God into the future and dissect it from the present, it will be of no effect in the world now. God's kingdom is here now, as well as being part of the not yet when it will be fully and finally established. The kingdom is the mustard plant growing in our own historical context today, and is on display through Christian communities that live out their picture of Christ the Lord of peace, and who incarnate as Christ's ministering hands and feet with people of no or little faith.

We need to foreshadow the coming kingdom through our lifestyles based on the likeness of Jesus, the one we follow and upon whom we model our lives.[7] The kingdom is in a continuous process of arriving now, and this is what we should frame our missional community identities upon. The kingdom will finally become completely manifest when a tipping point is reached and Jesus returns to renew the earth.

---

6 Matthew 6:10, NRSVA.
7 N. T. Wright, *How God Became King*, London: SPCK (2012), pp. 3-24.

Denominational identities

In the Western context the mainline Christian denominations he\
to form the identities of the churches and the people who belong to
them. Four of the main denominations in the UK are the Baptists,
Methodists, Anglicans and Roman Catholics. We could debate
whether others should be included, but at this stage I am not
seeking to do a detailed analysis. Each of these four ecclesiastical
bodies has what might be called an institutional identity that shapes
the way the people who associate with it may identify themselves –
as Anglican, Baptist, etc.

Ecclesiology as a discipline that seeks to define a church group's identity

Theologians often speak of ecclesiology, the study of how churches
construct their theological identities. In other words, they seek to
understand the beliefs and practices of a given denomination which
help to shape the identities of the people who belong to it.
Obviously these beliefs and practices come from particular pictures
of what Christ is like, and they take their identities from what they
perceive to be the core beliefs and practices that framed Christ's
identity.

Vatican II: Catholicism in an emerging multidirectional missional context

We can see how ecclesiastical bodies go about fine-tuning their
identities with reference to the Roman Catholic Church. Within the
context of the Roman Catholic Church, change often happens at the
top of the institution, although it also responds to changes that are
occurring at different levels as well. A major sea change occurred in
the early 1960s when the twenty-first ecumenical council known as
Vatican II was formally opened under the pontificate of Pope John
XXIII. The groundbreaking new openness expressed during the
time of the Vatican II Council was a key moment which enabled the
Catholic Church to begin to see itself in fresh ways. Veli-Matti
Karkainen has this to say about its significance in updating its

...menically, a radical new perspective was launched with Vatican II, which brought a new appreciation of other churches and their contribution to the Christian testimony. It was admitted that the other churches carry with them saving function – although less full than that of Rome – and are transmitters of the gifts of the Holy Spirit. The old dogma *extra ecclesiam nulla salus* ('outside the church there is no salvation') no longer applied exclusively to the Roman Church; the new openness toward other churches came to be expressed by the slogan *Una sancta ecclesia subsistit in* ('One holy church subsists in [the Roman Church]'). Lumen Gentium [Light to the nations] stresses that the Catholic Church 'recognizes that in many ways she is linked' with other Christian communities by a true union in the Holy Spirit. Rahner [an important Catholic theologian] expresses this beautifully, saying that in the Spirit 'all of us "know" something more simple, more true and more real than we can know or express at the level of our theological concepts'.[8]

Although Protestant and Evangelical Christians will take issue with the implication that the Catholic faith is the fullest expression of the universal true church of Christ, it is interesting how Vatican II obtained its more open universal spirit of acceptance of unity with other denominations, based on recognition of the unifying work of the Spirit among all Christians. The recognition in the quote above is that it is the Spirit who helps all of us to know we are all linked 'by a true union in the Holy Spirit', as Christians of all persuasions are united by the one love of God in Christ because the Spirit is at work in all of them. A fresh picture of God the Spirit, as unifier of

---

[8] Veli-Matti Karkkainen, *An Introduction to Ecclesiology*, Downers Grove: IVP (2002), p. 37.

all Christian denominations and persuasions, is, at least in theory since Vatican II, part of Roman Catholic belief and thought. This change in outlook is somewhat prophetic of what will need to take place if we are to see Christianity make a new impact in postmodern Western society.

The need for an ecumenical conversation

Before the kingdom of God can take root more deeply in our Western societies, it needs to be visibly lived out through Christian groups who gather around the one Christ whom they follow, the one Father who loves all peoples and the one Spirit who unites all peoples. If we are all mystically one in Christ, then surely we should also become one in reality. Surely the picture of God portrayed by Christian denominations and networks uniting all believers through the one Spirit will provide a picture of God's power that heals ruptured relationships. What is needed is a new engagement in cross-denominational conversation.

If Christ loves everyone equally so that Christians are all one, then why are our churches not more united cross-denominationally? It seems to me that we need to find ways to form meaningful partnerships where we work together in our multicultural society as examples of the love of the one Lord who unites us. This means we will need to intentionally gather together in conversations that seek to transcend our doctrinal differences and unite in the name of the one universal head of the body of Christ. This will portray a picture of God in answer to that question. Let us not be naïve: secular people do ask questions about the God we claim to love by pointing us to the seeming divisions that exist between Christian denominations and groups.

New labels for a new Protestantism: the rise of denominational labels and ecclesiastical identities

It is interesting to consider how our Protestant ecclesiastical labels actually came about. For example, the sixteenth-century Protestant Reformation in Germany started with Martin Luther's desire to bring reform to the Roman Catholic Church, of which he was a part in his early life as an Augustinian monk. Luther began with the conviction that he needed to cleanse the Roman Church of its corruptions. He ended up being excommunicated from it, which led to the framing of a new identity for the movement that followed. That movement identified itself as a protestation against Roman Catholic corruption and abuse of power. Hence Protestantism was born. The label that Protestant people put on themselves was meant to say what they were not: they were not Roman Catholics. This label became the narrative picture of God and drove Lutheran churches to form a new identity which was something other than Catholic. Many new churches sprung up, and labelled themselves in different ways as suited to their contextual needs. The church universal fragmented into a kind of niche market spiritual economy suited to the contextual needs of a variety of different groups.

Moreover, some Reformed churches in the UK today still hold strong views about the Roman Catholic Church, and even identify it with the Antichrist and the Beast of Revelation 13. It seems that the identities of some Reformed church groups are framed on the basis of what they are not, rather than what they are. As a consequence, they exist to resist the works of the devil and to keep their people separate from what they call 'the world', with its corrupting influences. The picture of God that informs groups like these is of a God who will soon intervene in the world, through the second coming of Jesus Christ, to punish the wicked and to take the just to heaven to dwell with Christ forever. The group identity portrayed is one that says, 'We are not like them.' God is said to have called such groups to exist in order to resist and protest against what they consider to be false Christian teachings, to which other Christian groups hold as well. There is a remnant theology where people in such groups think of themselves as a special elect group who follow Christ and have the true interpretation of sound Christian doctrines. Those who do not agree with their doctrines are not part of the elect. Hence we can see how a remnant theology can define a group's sphere and range of influence.

However, it is important to note that Reformed churches make up a smaller part of the Christian family in the UK today. My aim is not to criticise Reformed groups, but rather to note some basic elements that shape their identities. Moreover, most mainline western Evangelical churches trace their theological heritages back to the Reformation. They too give themselves labels to form their communities' identities. For example, the Methodist church began with the Wesley brothers who started out as ordained clergy. They, like Luther, did not intend to split the Methodist movement away from the Church of England. However, the emphasis on gospel preaching and the priority of gospel-based evangelism, largely among the working class, made conversion by new birth a key theme that formed their movement's identity. Most Evangelical churches take their identities from new birth theology. The Wesley brothers' gospel preaching led to them being shut away from the pulpits of the English church system as it was viewed as fanatical.

Methodists also became more radically identified with the Reformation emphasis on the priesthood of all believers. John Wesley set up lay Bible schools, through which lay preachers were trained and sent out to share the gospel. Gospel conversions, where people could be said to have been born again, traces its heritage back to the Wesleyan revival. This has been called the first great awakening by some Evangelical historians.

What was the picture of God that drove this movement? It was based on the conversion experience of new converts and then their ongoing experiences as believers who continued to enjoy God's presence in their lives. In the early Methodist picture of God, Christ was still active in the church and society, and people could attest to personal, experiential and life-transforming encounters with Him.

Identity as restoration of New Testament church life

The narrative picture of God conveyed in Wesleyan revivalism is of the Spirit of Christ being a real, dynamic encounter for converts, often pointing to a moment when God entered their lives as a felt presence. This gave licence to the view that emerged in the nineteenth century that churches needed to return to apostolic

Christianity as recorded in the book of Acts and the epistles of Paul. A more supernatural form of engagement with the still active, ascended Jesus through His Spirit was required. This came to be known in one movement called Churches of Christ, which insisted that the church needed to return to its New Testament, Acts-based Christianity.

In the early twentieth century, the arrival of Pentecostalism took much of its fuel from the ideas of restorationism, which were part of an undercurrent in the psyches of many Christians in the US. The picture of God during this movement of the Spirit was one where Christ's Spirit was expected to behave just as it did in the New Testament church. There are about 600 million Pentecostal/ Charismatic Christians in the world today. The huge and rapid conversions of people groups in the southern hemisphere as a result of this movement of the Spirit is staggering. Surely the living God is active, and His kingdom continues to come and is witnessing whole societies being transformed by the sheer numbers of those living in them who follow Christ.

Charismatic revival entered the Anglican Church during the late 1970s and 1980s through the initial influence of people like Michael Harper and the Fountain Trust, and later John Wimber, a charismatic leader from North America. From this root, an expression of a continued restorationism and revivalism has been expressed by the Anglican Holy Trinity Brompton church.

> ### Identity based on being Bible believers
>
> Church of God of Prophecy, UK
>
> 'We are an orthodox Bible-believing fellowship. This means we accept the Bible as the revealed Word of God: inspired, inerrant, and infallible. We therefore look to the Bible as our highest authority for principles governing doctrine, practice, organisation, and discipline. The Church of God of Prophecy is a Pentecostal church made up of Bible-believing Christians who are called by God to bring to mankind hope and life in Jesus Christ through the gospel message.'
>
> http://www.cogop.org.uk/

The evangelistic outreach strategies of many denominational and non-denominational churches in the UK have been significantly impacted by the Alpha course, which aims to teach the gospel to people. The course is based on a Trinitarian theology, where Christ is portrayed as our Saviour whom we must make a personal decision to accept, and where the baptism of the Holy Spirit is key.

The charismatic evangelical Alpha course sets the Trinity at the heart of Christian identity

The picture of God conveyed by the Alpha initiative is of God as three persons joined in one purpose to bring transformation into contemporary peoples' lives. This God is our Father, who loves us and wants us to join His family. He is our God who incarnated among us in Jesus Christ, who is the one who saves us and the one we need to follow. God is the Holy Spirit, who enables us to have an ongoing relationship with the living God throughout our lives. We can see once again that a variety of ways of picturing the God upon which our various churches base their social identities are founded on the ideals of those who started these movements. The Alpha movement bears some identifying characteristics with early Methodism, revivalism and restorationism. It certainly draws on the Pentecostal spiritual stream as well. Alpha shares its identity with the conviction that God is really present and active in Christian spiritual experiences. Most importantly, it emphasises the need for Christian identity to be based on Trinitarian theology. This emphasis offers a practical theological corrective to unbalanced ecclesial identities that some churches in the Free Church sector found their identities upon. Too often in their theology one or two persons of the Godhead are emphasised, rather than three. The result is that there is an imbalanced theology of God.

Conclusions

What I have wanted to achieve in this chapter is to highlight that Christian communities (churches and denominations) form their identities based on their picture of God. A group's picture of God

33

seeks to capture a dynamic portrait of what God is like. Our pictures of God frame our identities based on the stories we communicate to each other about Him. People in a Christian community do what they believe God wants them to do based on the dynamic stories they tell each other, which motivate their behaviours. It is important to have a balanced Trinitarian picture of God to help groups to frame their identities around the persons of the Father, Son and Holy Spirit (we will discuss why this is important in later chapters). Part of most missional church identities is a picture of the God who wants to reconcile the faith-seeker into His cosmic family.

All of our various Christian groups seem to share one conviction in common: that God is love. But the way we define that love is quite a different matter, as we will see. How might our pictures of God be adapted so that we can go beyond our ethnocentric commitments to a particular denomination's identity? How can we more widely join together through a new picture of God that has us all united in the love of the Christ who is the Lord of the one body to which we all belong?

We may point to some hopeful signs, as well as to some real challenges for us to do this together, in the Western context of a pluralistic multicultural society. In conversations I have had with some ethnic leaders there has been open hostility to any suggestion that different cultural expressions of Christianity, now present in Western society, should in any way work together. However, I have good friends in Black churches, Indian churches, Chinese churches, Polish churches, etc. who are seeking to build bridges and to get to know each other better. What is encouraging is that many migrant churches seek not just to fellowship more broadly with other Christians, but also to reach out to non-Christians from their own ethnic groups. If we are genuine in our desires to unite with brothers and sisters from other ethnic groups and cultures in Christ, then we must start to do some of the hard work to intentionally join together in some multicultural missional conversations and partnerships. We need to find ways of sharing a more common identity built on our shared rootedness in the body of the Lord Jesus Christ.

One suggestion is that God's mission needs to start with united Christian partnerships if we are to seek to bring non-believers into the kingdom of God in the Western context, a kingdom of which Christ is Lord, a united body made up of many tongues, peoples and nations, who in the book of Revelation are portrayed as worshipping around the throne of God.[9] God's mission (*missio Dei*) has to do with the great eternal purpose of the Trinity for all peoples to be united in God's love as one family cared for by one eternal Father, the Spirit as Mother and the Son as Brother to His followers.[10]

Our picture of God may become one where all people groups are being called together, as one missional people, to become part of the Trinity's eternal kingdom community. The picture of God as a missionary, who sent His Son into the world to bring the lost back into union in His family, is the primary narrative of this book. It is important to understand that when I talk about a Christian community having a picture of God which defines its beliefs and actions, I also include the stories its members tell themselves about who they are, where they came from and how they are going to engage in God's purposes within their non-Christian communities. The overall purpose of God's mission is to unite all peoples into the Trinitarian family. In other words, I am a Trinitarian theologian.

In later chapters, as we move towards defining the picture of the missionary God (*missio Dei* theology), we will need to obtain a deeper understanding of how this theology came about. It will be important to define terms suitable to our multicultural pluralistic context in the West. I believe we can do this best by using the metaphor of God's mission being to reconcile all multicultural peoples into the Trinity's family. I also want to emphasise that when I talk about Christian community, I mean places of friendship and communion between the varieties of peoples who make up the multicultural tapestry.

---

[9] Revelation 7:1-10.
[10] Ephesians 1:9-10.

If there is one vital lesson to take from the view of God as Father, Son and Spirit, it is that their co-existence is based on deep trust that frames their shared oneness in the being of God. Their inward and outward life together is based on naked transparency, vulnerability, complete trust in one another, and sacrificial commitment, which means they deeply share themselves with each other – without reservation.[11] Our communities need to start to frame their identities on this kind of communion, based on the picture of the persons of God united in sacrificial love. Our communities need to be identified by outsiders as places of deep, love-based fellowship and communion.

The Trinity is a Multicultural Trinity (MT), whose mission is to unite all peoples and cultures in the one body of the cosmic Christ.

It is important to remember as we progress through this volume that I include all ethnic groups in the West as part of our multicultural society. This includes the so-called 'new tribes' of Generation Y's young adults on the basis of the values and norms which define their numerously differing subcultures. In order to understand how such groups can come to appreciate who God is for them in relation to their own identity formation, we will take some time in the next chapter to consider how each gospel account framed its theological picture of Jesus to resonate with the particular contextual needs of the community for which each gospel was written. After all, the gospels are missional documents.

---

[11] See, for example, John 17:4-20. In this passage Christ prays to His Father that His disciples may enter into the relationship He has with His Father; described as the Father being 'in' Christ and Christ being 'in' the Father. This language of 'being in' has long been recognised by some thinkers to be a way that John seeks to portray the utter naked openness between Father and Son; because both know each other's naked inner selves to the depths of their mutual being God.

Chapter 2
Pictures of Christ in the synoptic gospels

Constructing images of Jesus that relate to community identities

It may be of no surprise to you that each of the three synoptic[12] gospels (Matthew, Mark and Luke) present their pictures of Jesus through different lenses, in order for the Jesus story to be contextually relevant to the Christian communities for which they were written. Some New Testament scholars speak of the gospels having been constructed to portray a picture of Jesus that was relevant to the life situations of their peoples. I would add that it is my belief that the authors were inspired by the Holy Spirit to do this so that the portrayals of Jesus they conveyed were true to His real-life beliefs and practices while He lived on the earth.

However, my conviction that the Holy Spirit ensured that the real Jesus of history was broadly captured by the gospel writers is not accepted by some gospel scholars. The New Testament scholar Dale Allison believes that the gospel accounts, including the sayings of Jesus, are largely based on distorted memories of Jesus' life and teachings. He contests that there is no stable picture of Jesus to be found in the gospels. For example, let's consider what he has to say about the human ability to confuse memories. He applies this to the life, teachings and events recorded for us in the synoptic gospels, and claims that we cannot hope to reconstruct the historical Jesus from these accounts:

---

[12] Synoptic means to 'see things together' and describes the three gospels as essentially telling a similar story of Jesus although they convey it in different ways.

We are apt to project present circumstances and biases onto our past experiences, assimilating our former selves to our present selves. We may, for example, assume that we once believed what we have believed only of late and distort our recall accordingly. 'Surely it must have been like this' readily becomes 'It was so.' Similarly, our moral judgments may amend our memories. We may confuse what we think ought to have occurred with what did occur.[13]

Allison goes on to say that this must be part of the explanation for why the different gospel accounts portray Jesus from different points of view, putting words into His mouth, making them say something quite different compared to the recorded uses in the other synoptic gospels.

The New Testament scholar Richard Bauckham does not agree with this kind of reasoning. Rather, he convincingly demonstrates that the original gospels probably had the names of eyewitnesses connected to the sayings and events of Jesus' ministry.[14] Near contemporaries to these eyewitnesses, who had not made contact with Jesus during His life, could visit these eyewitnesses and confirm the verity of their accounts. This makes great sense to me.

If the risen Christ was venerated as Lord (Yahweh) by the first Christians, as some important scholars suggest was the case from just after the resurrection, it is unthinkable that records of His sayings and doings would have been distorted easily. Indeed, there is no good reason to assume that this did happen, despite the voices of scholars who claim it did. I believe the common-sense view is that the first generation of believers ensured that the representation of the words and works of Jesus could be relied on as good approximations of what He actually did and said. The Jews were people of written books, and the early followers of Jesus are likely

---

[13] Dale C. Allison, *Constructing Jesus: Memory, Imagination and History*, Grand Rapids: SPCK (2010), p. 4.
[14] Richard Bauckham, *Jesus and the Eyewitnesses: The Gospels as Eyewitness Testimony*, Cambridge: Eerdmans (2006), pp. 1-38.

to have had the means to accurately record the life, sayings and works of Jesus. In my view, this means that the words, actions and events of Jesus' life are based on verifiable eyewitness testimony. They are theological accounts of his life and teachings rather than biographical histories of his life such as would be written by modern historical biographers.[15] Early Christian writers asserted that the records of the gospels were genuine and reliable records of Jesus life and teachings.

Allison provides an interesting insight with regard to how human beings construct their identities, individually and corporately:

> Individuals transmute memories into meaningful patterns that advance their agendas. Collectives do likewise. We remember publicly in order to persuade, to justify ourselves, and to explain current circumstances. In other words, memories are a function of self-interest, and we instinctively review them in order to help maintain 'a meaningful sense of self-identity.'[16]

Although I would not go as far as Allison in suggesting that the early church distorted the Jesus memories and their conveyances of them, I do agree that our memories of what Jesus said and did can be used selectively by our Christian communities to construct a picture of what Jesus was like. I would say that the gospel writers acted as editors who selected stories, sayings and happenings from Jesus' life in order to construct their gospels to meet the contextual needs of the communities they wrote for. This does mean that the Jesus stories have the authors' theological slants guiding what they wanted to say about Christ, but I believe they did this under the guidance of the Spirit of Jesus. In a special sense, they did not distort the Jesus of history, making Him into somebody He was not; rather, the Spirit guided them to structure their stories to offer a portrayal

---

[15] Bauckham, *Jesus and the Eyewitnesses*, pp. 1-38.
[16] Allison, *Constructing Jesus*, p. 6.

of Him that would inform identities, beliefs and missional actions in their localised contexts.

The New Testament scholar Michael White has written an interesting liberal account of his views about the Jesus of history. His book is entitled *Scripting Jesus: The Gospels in Rewrite.*[17] He comments about the fourfold gospel narratives (Matthew, Mark, Luke and John):

> The Gospels as we now have them are not direct or neutral accounts of Jesus. Nor do they claim to be. They do not operate under modern conceptions of writing history, nor were there 'four guys on a street corner'. Instead, they are early attempts to weave the various materials, whether oral or written, into a narrative about Jesus for a particular audience in a particular context.[18]

It is important to note that each of the synoptic gospels portrays different aspects of the personality and character of Jesus to the communities for which they were written, so that these communities could meaningfully portray the Jesus of their faith to those who as yet did not have faith in Him. This means that we can reconstruct from each gospel the characteristics of their communities, based on the picture of Jesus each gospel conveys.

These pictures of Jesus helped construct the missional outreach of each community. So what can we learn about the people and the communities from the picture of Jesus that is conveyed in the three synoptic gospels? There is little doubt that the very term 'gospel' (meaning 'good news') implies that the authors wrote in order that the communities could engage in God's mission locally. This must be a realistic view to adopt, given that present-day missional communities also gather around the stories of Jesus that best describe their mission endeavours.

---

[17] L. Michael White, *Scripting Jesus: The Gospels in Rewrite*, New York: HarperOne (2011).
[18] White, *Scripting Jesus*, p. 11.

The Jesus of Matthew's gospel community

The Christian community that Matthew's gospel was written for was almost certainly made up of Jewish believers. An early tradition suggests that the sayings found in Matthew's gospel were first recorded in the Hebrew language. Whether this really was the case is impossible to determine. It seems more likely that the gospel was written in Greek and that the Jewish believers were Hellenists. The Hellenist party is mentioned in the book of Acts.[19] This particular group was made up of the many Jews who had settled around the Roman Empire, such as in Rome, Philippi and Asia Minor. They communicated using the common Greek tongue with their Gentile contemporaries. The writer of the gospel portrays a very Jewish picture of Jesus to followers in the Jewish diaspora who lived around the Mediterranean basin.

The picture of Jesus in this gospel is built around what was meant to be read as a new Torah given to the new Moses – Jesus. There are five clear teaching sections in the gospel, probably understood by Jewish readers to imply that Jesus was delivering a new Torah of five books like the Pentateuch, fit for the arrival of the kingdom of God, which Jesus the Son of David was ushering in. There are some common portrayals of Jesus in this gospel that would have made these Jewish Christians sit up and pay attention to His words and works.

First of all, Jesus fulfils the prophecies about the long-expected Messiah who will usher in the eternal reign of Yahweh. Christ is particularly identified with the suffering servant of Isaiah 53[20] and the Son of Man figure talked of in Daniel 7.[21] In the case of the Son of Man figure, Jesus directly connects Himself with this being who, according to Daniel 7, would be the eternal ruler of the kingdom of God which would replace all earthly kingdoms. Jesus is pictured as an eternal figure who comes from the 'ancient of days', who is identified with the heavenly Father in Matthew's gospel. The

---

[19] Acts 6:1.
[20] Matthew 8:17.
[21] Matthew 24:15.

41

picture is of this heavenly Son of Man having been sent by the Father to inaugurate the eternal kingdom of God. The Jewish Christians are to accept their Messiah as their king.

Secondly, the gospel uses a particular formula when it introduces each of the five teaching sections. In Matthew 5, Jesus is said to sit down on the mountain before He delivers his teaching on the moral principles of the Christian life. Once He has completed His teaching He stands and moves on from the mountain to another place. The portrayal of Jesus, as the prophet like Moses in this passage, would have spoken volumes to Jews. Jesus, just like Moses, delivers the laws of Yahweh from the mountain. The big difference between the account of Moses giving the law to the Israelites and the story of the Sermon on the Mount is that Jesus sits down, delivering the new kingdom laws as a king who is authorised to do so. In the story of the giving of the law, found in the Torah, Moses is given the law by God. He does not declare it like Jesus the messianic king does, who was recognised to have authority that no man had ever had.[22] The picture of Jesus, the Son of David, is of a Messiah with heavenly authority, like that of Yahweh himself.

---

[22] Matthew 7:28-29.

Thirdly, Jesus is recognised as the Son of God.[23] As Son of God, He is also called 'Lord' by His disciples. The use of the word 'Lord' in Matthew is probably meant to be understood as if the followers of Jesus are addressing Him as Yahweh, or Yahweh's special Son.

Fourthly, after Jesus' resurrection, Matthew 28:16-20 speaks of Him appearing to His disciples on a mount once again. His followers fall down and worship Him as their Lord. Jesus is offered the worship that is only due to God Himself. Based on this deep passionate devotion for Jesus the Messiah, the Jewish Christian community for which the gospel was written is commanded to make disciples of all nations. This is significant in terms of the Old Testament prophecies that were associated with the Messiah. In Psalm 2, the nations are pictured as subject to the Lord's anointed. This picture of Jesus the Messiah frames the identity of this Jewish Christian community around its mission to make disciples of all nations, so that these nations may worship Jesus as the king of Yahweh's kingdom.

What we discover in Matthew's gospel is a strong messianic portrayal of the divine Son of God, who calls His disciples to baptise new followers in the name of the Father, Son and Holy Spirit. The wording of this Matthean baptismal formula gives co-equality to the three persons of the Trinity, although the word 'Trinity' is not used, of course. The Jewish messianic community of Matthew's gospel has been sent on the mission of the living resurrected Jesus, who will be with them to the end of the age. When He returns, His messengers (angels) will gather these disciples together to worship at the mountain of the house of the Lord (Mount Zion).

The Jesus of Mark's gospel community

The Jesus portrayed in Mark's gospel is first of all of Jesus 'the Son of God'.[24] This opening phrase is vital to understand as it speaks volumes about the social context of the Christian groups for which it was written. Early church tradition seems to rightly assign the

---

[23] Matthew 27:54.
[24] Mark 1:1.

43

origin of this gospel to Rome. The writer, called Mark, was possibly the Mark over whom Paul and Barnabas fell out because of his youth and inexperience.[25] Papias, an early Christian writer, suggests that Mark wrote down the preaching of the apostle Peter in the form of what we now call Mark's gospel. I feel fairly comfortable with these origins of place and authorship for the gospel; it contains Latinisms in the Greek text, which suggests Rome as the location of the Christian communities for which it was produced.

Calling Jesus 'the Son of God' was of great significance to dwellers in Rome, given that Augustus Caesar, and Roman emperors who followed him, were portrayed to be 'sons of the gods.' It is as if Mark is saying that Jesus Christ was not just one of many sons of the gods, offspring of the numerous gods, but that He is the one true Son of the one true Christian God. Hence the central theme of Mark's gospel has to do with the conviction that Jesus is divine, and therefore demands worship that supersedes claims of any other pretenders who demand personal worship from their citizens. I believe this is at the heart of the picture of the Christ of Mark's community.

Secondly, Mark asserts that the God we find in Christ is not like those of the Roman Empire. Jesus does not exercise coercive power to dominate the lives of His followers. Instead He gives people free licence to follow Him and to learn from Him. He does not rule like the Roman rulers, who from time to time require people to offer sacrifices to their images. The picture of Jesus for Mark's gospel community is of a saviour sent to deliver His people by redemptive sacrifice, rescuing them from the would-be gods of the empire.

Thirdly, Mark asserts that many were blind to who Jesus was. His own Jewish compatriots did not recognise Him as their Messiah. The power-hungry empire was also blind to this messianic king who suffered on a cross reserved for criminals. How can one who suffered a criminal's death be the 'Son of God'? How can such a one be the subject of worship? Yet Mark's gospel pictures Jesus as

---

[25] Acts 15:36-41.

44

one who remains hidden to those who do not receive Him or receive the new spiritual insight about His true identity, as Messiah and Lord. The picture of God's kingdom offered to Mark's gospel community is one which is not of this world, but of the world to come, over which the Son of God will reign.

Fourthly, the picture of Jesus in Mark is of a dynamic activist. The gospel portrays Jesus engaging in immediate missional activities to push back the powers of evil and to rescue people so that they can become part of God's kingdom. The missional community of Mark's gospel must also have valued evangelistic activism, where its people robustly and bravely sought to share the good news about Jesus, 'the Son of God', with all who would listen. It is of little surprise that this gospel of action proves to be popular with younger adults, who long to change the world by evangelising it with the good news of the Son of God.

Fifthly, Mark's gospel community was focused on sharing the good news of the kingdom of God, to which Jesus offered access. In this kingdom there would be no more abuse of power, no more torture, slavery and subjugation. Rather, God's Son would walk alongside those who had accepted His call, helping them to find their destinies in the kingdom that would be based on Yahweh's reign of peace.

The Jesus of Luke's gospel community

Luke's gospel community's picture of Jesus is in many ways the most spectacular of the three synoptic gospels. In it we find the Holy Spirit at work, from the moment of Christ's divine conception in Mary's womb until the resurrection, where Jesus promised the disciples they would receive the Holy Spirit, after He had ascended to His Father in heaven. As we will see later, the picture presented in Luke–Acts[26] has the missionary churches in Philippi (the most

---

[26] It is accepted by some important New Testament scholars that the writer of Luke's gospel was the same person who wrote the book of Acts.

likely Christian community the gospel was written for in my view[27]) being guided by the missionary Spirit of Jesus to continue His words and deeds among the people of Macedonia and Greece. The picture of Jesus in Luke is based on the idea of Jesus completing His predetermined mission by His sacrifice in Jerusalem. This then led to the coming of His Spirit to establish His kingdom, into which believers enter when they embrace faith in Christ.

Secondly, Luke's gospel community presents a picture of Jesus as the universal Lord of all nations. Starting from Jesus' mission among His own people, the book of Acts extends it to all the Gentile nations. It is almost impossible to understand Luke's gospel without understanding the message of Acts as well, as it was almost certainly written by the same author. In Luke's gospel, Gentiles are also the focus of Christ's mission. We do not find the same emphasis on this in the gospel of Matthew. The Christian community in Philippi is predominantly a Gentile one. The picture of Jesus, for this missional community, is that Christ wants all peoples to worship Him as Lord. The strong theme of discipleship in the book demonstrates that believers are to follow in His footsteps, modelling their ministries on that of Jesus. The ministry of Jesus characterised in Luke–Acts is expressed as His followers continue His words and works. The church needs to engage with Christ's

---

[27] The reason I believe Philippi is the most likely location is because in Acts 16:6-10 one of the famous 'we' passages is inserted by the writer, indicating that the author went with Paul to Philippi and remained with him there. When Paul goes south into Greece, the 'we' passage ends. I believe Luke stayed in Philippi, and the fact that his gospel and Acts show a strong regard for the role of women among Jesus' disciples fits with an attempt by Luke to contextualise the gospel to suit the situation in Philippi, located as it was in Macedonia. Macedonia was the only region in the Greco-Roman Empire where women had a closer to equal status with men, being allowed to trade for themselves and own their own businesses. Hence I favour the writing of some of Luke, at least, having taken place there, owing to Luke having lived in that region for a while with the newly founded church there after Paul travelled south. It is quite possible that Luke helped plant the church in Philippi and was Paul's missional agent there to oversee the developments of this new community.

Spirit, continuing to follow Him as they are guided to pursue His mission until the kingdom has fully come.

Thirdly, Luke focuses on the importance of women in Jesus' earthly ministry. Women were among His disciples. Women went bravely and fearlessly ahead of His male disciples to His tomb after the crucifixion. Women had an important part to play in the proclamation of the coming kingdom of God. Interestingly, it was only in Philippi, in Macedonia, that women had more or less equal status with men: they could trade, run a business and engage in mercantile ventures. The picture of Christ offered by Luke to his gospel community is one where women are more equal to men. Christ is not a patriarch who puts women in their cultural place, but rather He values them as His disciples.

Luke's gospel is also well known for its concern for justice and mercy for outcasts. Jesus declares in the Nazareth Manifesto[28] that He has been sent to proclaim liberty to outcasts. The mission of Jesus brings the kingdom of God into society in order to transform its peoples and its structures, to become inclusive of all. The picture of Christ in this gospel displays God's mercy as the core narrative that describes the reign of God. The reign of God is to bring about an equal society which is not based on partiality, and where the rich are not favoured to the detriment of the poor and vulnerable.

Constructing the identities of our Christian communities

Each of the gospels clearly portrays a picture of Jesus' character, values, beliefs and practices that is suited to the contextual needs of each gospel community. Our own Christian communities have also actively been part of the formation of the identities of their people, based on a picture of Christ. The sociologist Manuel Castells speaks of how we all have a part to play in the construction of the identifying attributes and values of our own communities:

---

[28] Luke 4:14-20.

It is easy to agree on the fact that, from a sociological perspective, all identities are constructed. The real issue is how, from what, by whom, and for what. The construction of identities uses building materials from history, from geography, from biology, from productive and reproductive institutions, from collective memory and from personal fantasies, from power apparatuses and religious revelations. But individuals, social groups, and societies process all these materials, and rearrange their meaning, according to social determinations and cultural projects that are rooted in their social structure, and in their space/time framework.[29]

I propose that our Christian communities need to continue in a process of constructing their communal identities by becoming aware of the picture/s of God upon which they base the behaviours and beliefs of their people. This will call for critical self-awareness of leaders who intentionally engage in identifying the picture/s of Christ that construct the identities of their communities. Communities will also greatly benefit from having others outside of their community to help them identify the picture of God which drives their behaviour. Obviously, our own special cultural contexts are founded on our local contexts, and on the joys and challenges our people face within them. These experiences will also inform the needs that our communities seek to be fulfilled, with reference to their particular picture/s of God.

People tell themselves stories based on what helps them to frame their identities. The communities to which we belong offer believers meaning in the context of their real-life situations. Becoming aware of the needs that drive us to seek a particular picture of Christ will develop our awareness of the picture of Christ upon which our communities are founded. As self-awareness increases, it will help us to engage in a self-critical process of growth, where we seek to

---

[29] Manuel Castells, *The Power of Identity: The Information Age - Economy, Society, and Culture, volume 2*, Chichester: Wiley-Blackwell (2004), p. 7.

journey with the living Jesus of the Spirit as we continue to construct our identities.

The various gospel portrayals of Jesus will relate in important ways to our own contextual needs and will help us to keep growing, to stay healthy and to respond to changes in our society, which continuously impact us. Luke–Acts suggests that our communities need to maintain continuous dialogue with the Christ of the Spirit. It is the Spirit who brings Christ into our lives, addressing our needs for an authentic, robust faith that can cope effectively with life's stresses and challenges. A community's critical self-awareness is enhanced when it compares its picture of Christ to pictures of Christ held by other communities. We will address the question of how to help our communities to engage in developing their pictures of God in chapter 10.

> **Identity based on sharing Jesus as the good news!**
>
> Christian Church (Disciples of Christ) – USA and Canada
>
> 'Our Identity
>
> We are Disciples of Christ, a movement for wholeness in a fragmented world. As part of the one body of Christ, we welcome all to the Lord's Table as God has welcomed us.
>
> Our Vision
>
> To be a faithful, growing church that demonstrates true community, deep Christian spirituality and a passion for justice – Micah 6:8.
>
> Our Mission
>
> To be and to share the Good News of Jesus Christ, witnessing, loving and serving from our doorsteps 'to the ends of the earth' – Acts 1:8.'
>
> http://disciples.org/our-identity/our-mission-vision-and-confession/

Our tree and the trees of God's forest

A prophetic picture was given to me about 15 years ago. I was portrayed as communicating the word of God to the creatures in a dark forest, which at first was not illuminated by the light of Christ. However, as I continued to communicate the Scriptures to the

49

creatures of this forest, many different-shaped eyes reflected back the light of the living Christ. This kept happening until the whole forest of God's diverse creatures was full of God's light. It was the eyes of the creatures that illuminated it, as they shone forth the glory of the inner Christ. Darkness was expelled.

I believe this picture had to do with what forms my own spiritual and missional passion, to see many different people groups and cultures (multicultural peoples in the West) brought to a united faith in God. The kingdom of God will be fully and finally ready to be established when all are joined together as one people of God, because the same Christ is worshipped by all. I perceive this picture to relate to teaching ministries, like my own and those of others, through which God is involved in the same ministry throughout the world. It is part of a meta-paradigm, in other words, in which I believe we all have a part to play.

Since I first received this prophetic word, it has been wonderful to experience the fellowship that comes from being part of an expanding missional movement in my context in the West, where many others are seeking to discover what Christ is calling His people to communicate about their God to secular society. As we share with others in our multicultural societies pictures of God that are centred on the living Christ of the Spirit, it will inevitably lead, in my view, to the uniting of different peoples as one family in the kingdom of God. This is the goal of *missio Dei* that God's kingdom comes on earth as it is in heaven. This is part of the Lord's kingdom prayer, which we are all called to pray in common, despite our cultural and racial differences. I believe that the call of God to the Western (and worldwide) churches is to engage in the Multicultural Trinity's mission, to unite all tongues, peoples and nations under the loving reign of the one God and Father of us all. Let us not forget that multicultural society in the West includes natives and emerging postmodern new tribes and their subcultures.

Another way of talking about this forest is to consider it to be made up of numerous different kinds of trees that all equally belong to God's one kingdom forest. The people who live in each of these multi-variant trees know their tree the best. They understand how their tree grows, they know its bark, its wood, its fruit and its leaves. However, they may be limited to understanding their own tree, without knowing any of the other trees in the forest. They may not have had the motivation or courage to walk the footpaths of the forest to get to know other trees and their dwellers.

This analogy may be applied to our multicultural society. We know our own churchmanship quite well, but we are not comfortable to walk on the forest footpaths to get to know other trees. All trees are trees, even if they may have some different characteristics from our own tree. The different trees produce their own fruit and have their own bark and leaves. They convey a picture somewhat different from our own trees. These other trees are no less good to live in than our own tree, for their particular dwellers. They all draw from the nutrients provided by the one and the same forest of God. As we come to accept that different ethnic cultural groups define their own Christian communities, sharing some things in common in the forest of God's kingdom, we and they may be motivated to go out and to try the fruits of these different trees.

They are all God's trees, but they may seem different to us, just as there is a difference between the fruit of a conker tree and that of an apple tree. However, as we get to know each tree, we will hopefully discover that God is at work in a diverse forest of many different multicultural expressions of what it means to be a tree of God. When we start to get to know the people of each tree better, we also may discover fresh ways that their picture of God can help to inform our group's identity. There are faith-seekers, and some who do not realise that they are seeking faith, who as yet have no tree to call their own. However, the people who walk among the different multicultural expressions of Christian communities that make up Western society are likely to be attracted to the communities that portray a picture of Christ which is most relevant to their particular needs. The vision of the forest that became full of Christ's light symbolises the multicultural societies in which Westerners live. It is also representative of all of the world cultures that form the rich diversity of the world God is reshaping to inhabit His kingdom forest.

What I raise here is the wonderful opportunity that the numerous cultural expressions of Christian faith can offer to each other, and which can impact the lives of peoples in our multicultural society. Each of our Christian communities can offer a picture of Christ that is appropriate to the needs of a given group, or subcultural group, of people who live and walk among us. Each of our communities conveys a picture of God that, if it is truly Christian, will have the living Jesus of the Spirit transforming people's lives as they get to know the God who lives in our communities. To my mind, what matters most to all of our expressions of the body of Christ will be that each builds its identity on belonging to the family of the MT. The MT is the kingdom forest, the eternal family to which all peoples, tongues and nations need to belong.

The synoptic gospels, in the context of the multicultural Greco–Roman Empire of the first century AD, provided pictures of the one resurrected and ascended Lord who could meet the human need to rediscover its identity in the image of Christ. Each community's local context, in God's multicultural forest, has trees that are best suited to the people with whom God calls us to missionally engage, as we meet them regularly on the footpaths.

We will consider later the contribution of John's gospel to the picture of the divine Christ. It, too, was produced to provide a picture of Christ to the Hellenist Jewish community of the late first century AD. Its contributions have much to offer to my vision of MT, and how MT can enhance the partnerships we form with other peoples from other cultures now living in the West. The world is on our doorstep. God calls us to walk among the people of the world and to get to know each other better, so that we can better see Christ pictured in one another. The MT's purpose is to reconcile all dwellers of the multicultural forest so that all the tree dwellers may live at peace with one another. This is MT's mission, around which I believe our differing ethnic and postmodern tribe-like Christian communities need to gather, because we are all part of Trinity's eternal family.

Conclusion

This chapter has focused on the importance of the pictures or images of Christ upon which participants frame their identities. In pastoral psychology, the identity of the Christian who is being transformed into the likeness of the living Christ of the Spirit is of paramount importance. Christ came not only to save humanity but also to restore the image of God in humankind.

In the following chapter we will consider how the image of Christ may be said to frame Christian identity in each of our communities.

Chapter 3
Communities made in the image of Christ

The previous chapter focused on the variety of pictures of Jesus that the synoptic gospels provided for their target communities. The gospels were essentially missional documents, designed to enable local Christian communities throughout the Empire to communicate the good news of Jesus.

The question may be in your mind, 'Is there actually one picture of Christ which we can all use as a benchmark?' We are His followers, so surely we should become like the prototype disciple – Jesus. I hope I did enough in the previous chapter to indicate that there is a real Jesus behind the various portrayals of His life and teachings. To bring out the real Jesus, as suited to the communities the gospels were produced for, various facets of His ministry were emphasised by the gospel writers. Any person is hugely complex, and so is their story. Jesus the Son of God has to be the most complex figure in human history to understand and portray.

When writing about the life of a key leader who has passed away, it is possible to come up with a variety of perspectives of what that leader was like, what they believed, did and said, particularly when more than one author writes about them. However, the person who is written about was a real person. Here is the nub of the challenge: the story of somebody is not the person themselves. The story seeks to represent something about them that captures them in a certain light. Hopefully, what is written by different authors will have baseline agreements about key facets that defined the person. However, we inevitably put our own interpretations on those we write about, because what we write is coloured by our personality, our culture, our context, and so on. In all of these ways, we may say that it is impossible for a story to be a person. What we have are snapshots of a person called Jesus coloured by all these factors, and more besides.

So how can we really have an accurate picture of what Jesus was like? The key difference between the variable pictures of Jesus in the gospels and accounts of famous men and women is that Jesus Christ is still alive. Moreover, Christians believe that Jesus Christ communicates through the gospels by illuminating, through the Spirit, facets of His life and sayings suited to the contexts of His contemporary followers. This is obviously an article of faith, but my own experiences, and that of millions of other Christians, is of authentic, verifiable encounters with Christ through His Spirit. Based on this conviction, I believe the resurrected and ascended Lord has proved that He is at work in my life, through the influence of Scripture and through others, and that the Spirit of Jesus works with my spirit to communicate deeply with me at the core of my inner being.

In this deep core, Christ's face shines, and His inner face of grace[30] transforms our inner selves to motivate our words, actions and behaviours towards others as if Christ Himself were communicating through our visible lives and experiences.

Christ is literally alive on a deep, mystical level within His followers. The inner conversation that goes on between our own spirits and the Spirit of Jesus transforms us into His likeness.[31] The role of the gospels is to provide us with inspiration about the pictures of Jesus they contain, guided as the gospel writers were by His Spirit. The role of others, whose outer lives are being motivated to reflect the inner Spirit of Jesus at work in their hearts, is yet another way in which a picture of Jesus is portrayed. Because Christians all belong to one body of Christ, with Christ as its guiding head, each of us carries part of Christ within ourselves. God provides differing gifts of Christ to each of us to help us discover the one Lord who motivates each of us to make our own unique contributions to each other and of the Christ portrayed through our

---

[30] 2 Corinthians 4:1-6.
[31] 2 Corinthians 3:18.

55

own life stories. Transformation into Christ's likeness is the work of a lifetime. These are the articles of faith that we need to understand the spiritually alive Jesus who inhabits each of our hearts. We are the picture of Christ's face that shines in our own hearts, which also transforms our faces to shine with His presence through our behaviour to others (see 2 Corinthians 3:1–4:6). God's people are the face, hands and feet of Christ's body, sent out to convey a picture of Jesus to the world. The apostle Paul makes this very point to the Corinthian believers:

> Are we beginning to commend ourselves again? Surely we do not need, as some do, letters of recommendation to you or from you, do we? You yourselves are our letter, written on our hearts, to be known and read by all; and you show that you are a letter of Christ, prepared by us, written not with ink but with the Spirit of the living God, not on tablets of stone but on tablets of human hearts.[32]

Paul's point is that the Holy Spirit is engaged on Christ's behalf in their innermost spirits, jointly authoring their life stories to tell the Jesus story to others. As Anthony Boison and Charles Gerkin argued,[33] they are living human documents whose life stories are co-authored with Christ, so that they can display a picture of Christ to others through their words and deeds. They are the letters of recommendation delivered, as it were, to those who as yet do not know Christ, in order to introduce Christ to faith-seekers in a favourable manner. Paul continues:

> Such is the confidence that we have through Christ towards God. Not that we are competent of ourselves to claim anything as coming from us; our competence is from God, who has made us competent to be ministers of a new covenant, not of letter but of spirit; for the letter kills, but the Spirit gives life.

---

[32] 2 Corinthians 3:1-3.

[33] Charles V. Gerkin, *The Living Human Document: Re-visioning Pastoral Counseling in a Hermeneutical Mode*, USA: Abingdon Press (1984).

> Now if the ministry of death, chiselled in letters on stone tablets, came in glory so that the people of Israel could not gaze at Moses' face because of the glory of his face, a glory now set aside, how much more will the ministry of the Spirit come in glory? For if there was glory in the ministry of condemnation, much more does the ministry of justification abound in glory! Indeed, what once had glory has lost its glory because of the greater glory; for if what was set aside came through glory, much more has the permanent come in glory![34]

Paul challenges his readers at this point to recognise that Moses, the ancient leader of God's people Israel, quite literally had his face shine with the radiance of Yahweh's glory when he came down from the mountain where he had met with God. The Ten laws that had been written by the finger of God on stone tablets were hard and unmalleable, yet still it was clear that God's love shone out on Moses' face, evident for all to see. Paul argues that the glory that is to shine out of our Christian stories, through our lives, is 'permanent', and comes with even more remarkable manifestations of Christ's glory than Moses had. Hence each of the Corinthian believers' stories would even more powerfully convey a picture of the love of God found in Christ to the pagan world than Moses had to the Israelites.

This is the reality that each of us is also to experience of the real living Christ, who will shine through our faces. 'Face' in the ancient Semite sense represented the visual display of a person's emotions, intentions, moods and characters. This is a good piece of concrete logic, given that our faces convey the most about how we feel, as body language experts tell us today. Only seven per cent of what we communicate is conveyed to others by our words; the other 93 per cent is conveyed through our tone of voice, facial expressions, body language, etc. The whole of our physical being conveys meaning to others, speaking volumes about what Christ is like, narrated as if our whole person were communicating Christ's

---

[34] 2 Corinthians 3: 4-11.

transformative incarnational presence through us. The reason why the preached word has less impact on postmodern young people is that it only deals with seven per cent of communication, whereas the communication of the meaning of Christ that will really impact them needs the seven per cent plus the other 93 per cent of real relationships with God's people, with whom they can have friendships in the ordinary rounds of daily life. The question is, are we forming deep friendships with the young adults of Generation Y?

This is why Generations Y and Z prefer to share life together in this way, as they need friendships with real people who live in the real world. Missional churches really need to stop assuming that meetings in a sacred building are what counts as most important; rather, people of the Christian community need to live incarnationally, alongside secular people in their neighbourhoods.

John Drane makes the point that from the 1960s onwards, people stopped going to churches for their spiritual answers because the people in those churches were not in touch with the real questions of ordinary people as they struggled to make sense of their evolving identities in the world.[35] It is through our physical beings that we convey a picture of Christ to others.

> Since, then, we have such a hope, we act with great boldness, not like Moses, who put a veil over his face to keep the people of Israel from gazing at the end of the glory that was being set aside. But their minds were hardened. Indeed, to this very day, when they hear the reading of the old covenant, that same veil is still there, since only in Christ is it set aside. Indeed, to this very day whenever Moses is read, a veil lies over their minds; but when one turns to the Lord, the veil is removed. Now the Lord is the Spirit, and where the Spirit of the Lord is, there is freedom. And all of us, with unveiled faces, seeing the

---

[35] John Drane, *Do Christians Know How to be Spiritual? The Rise of New Spirituality and the Mission of the Church,* London: Darton Longman and Todd (2005), chapter 1.

glory of the Lord as though reflected in a mirror, are being transformed into the same image from one degree of glory to another; for this comes from the Lord, the Spirit.[36]

The Spirit of the inner Christ reflects the image of Jesus to us, deeply within our interior, spiritual recesses. This will be as real to us as anything we experience in the physical, exterior world. We are to convey the image and likeness of Jesus to the people with whom we interact in our communities. Jesus' face shines within our hearts:

Therefore, since it is by God's mercy that we are engaged in this ministry, we do not lose heart. We have renounced the shameful things that one hides; we refuse to practise cunning or to falsify God's word; but by the open statement of the truth we commend ourselves to the conscience of everyone in the sight of God. And even if our gospel is veiled, it is veiled to those who are perishing. In their case the god of this world has blinded the minds of the unbelievers, to keep them from seeing the light of the gospel of the glory of Christ, who is the image of God. For we do not proclaim ourselves; we proclaim Jesus Christ as Lord and ourselves as your slaves for Jesus' sake. For it is the God who said, 'Let light shine out of darkness', who has shone in our hearts to give the light of the knowledge of the glory of God in the face of Jesus Christ.[37]

We, present-day followers of the living Christ, are spiritually vivified by His inner face, shining the glory of the Son of God to a fallen world of hurting peoples. We are being transformed from one degree of glory to another as we journey with the living Jesus throughout our lives. We are His face, His hands and His feet, sent out to show love, mercy and compassion, to heal the broken-hearted, to heal wounds and to release captives from the powers of darkness.

---

[36] 2 Corinthians 3:12-18.
[37] 2 Corinthians 4:1-6.

Imago Dei and *imago Christi*

Humankind was made in the *imago Dei* ('image of God') according to Genesis 1:26-27. This *imago Dei* was distorted by humanity's descent into sin and evil. God now provides us with a deep inner vivification of our spirits to be transformed by the *imago Christi* that shines in our hearts ('image of Christ'). The inner presence of the Spirit of Christ will be tested by each of us, in our Christian communities, through comparison with the Christ pictured in the gospels and other Scriptures, as well as with the Christ reflected by one another. We become like the living Lord, because He is alive and transforming our rebellious inner selves into the likeness of the one true man, made in God's image, Jesus Christ. Paul writes of Christ:

> He is the image of the invisible God, the firstborn of all creation; for in him all things in heaven and on earth were created, things visible and invisible, whether thrones or dominions or rulers or powers – all things have been created through him and for him. He himself is before all things, and in him all things hold together. He is the head of the body, the church; he is the beginning, the firstborn from the dead, so that he might come to have first place in everything. For in him all the fullness of God was pleased to dwell, and through him God was pleased to reconcile to himself all things, whether on earth or in heaven, by making peace through the blood of his cross.[38]

Humans will be transformed into the image of Christ if people are open to more than the rational preached word of Christ. We need to be open to all of Christ by opening our deepest hidden selves to the light of His shining face. This is radical spirituality which requires of us a new form of bravery, where we do not segment Christ into the logical categories of what we do on Sunday, or at house group, etc. Rather, Christ's Spirit needs to be let into

---

[38] Colossians 1:15-20.

every room in our inner houses, including our darkest rooms and cupboards, so that we might be fully vulnerable to Him. Theologian Stuart Murray identifies core values which make Anabaptist Christians distinct by the radical call to live the life which Jesus modelled in the ordinary rounds of His ministry, recorded in the gospels. He paints a radical view of what Christian values need to include. I recommend his book.[39]

In this vulnerability, giving Christ access to our darkest memories, God's people will be transformed into the likeness of Christ, who reveals what the Father and the Spirit are like. In what follows, I argue for the radical spirituality of becoming like Jesus, which means that we will be the picture of Christ's face of grace shining in our local communities. The *imago Dei* and the *imago Christi* are in fact the *imago Trinitatis* ('image of the Trinity'). In other words, humanity is made in the image of God's community, designed to live in Trinity's community. Indeed, we do not exist as real persons in our own right unless we live in meaningful relationships with others, because a person is defined as a real self only when he or she has other selves to define themselves in relation to (see chapter 7). The *imago Christi* is what we, His disciples, are to model our lives on. The *imago Christi* reveals what God the Trinity is like.

We all need to share the same attitude which Christ had:

> If then there is any encouragement in Christ, any consolation from love, any sharing in the Spirit, any compassion and sympathy, make my joy complete: be of the same mind, having the same love, being in full accord and of one mind. Do nothing from selfish ambition or conceit, but in humility regard others as better than yourselves. Let each of you look not to your own interests, but to the interests of others. Let the same mind be in you that was in Christ Jesus,
> who, though he was in the form of God,

---

[39] Stuart Murray, *The Naked Anabaptist: The Bare Essentials of a Radical Faith*, Milton Keynes: Paternoster (2011), pp. 70-92.

did not regard equality with God
as something to be exploited,
but emptied himself,
taking the form of a slave,
being born in human likeness.
And being found in human form,
he humbled himself
and became obedient to the point of death –
even death on a cross.
Therefore God also highly exalted him
and gave him the name
that is above every name,
so that at the name of Jesus
every knee should bend,
in heaven and on earth and under the earth,
and every tongue should confess
that Jesus Christ is Lord,
to the glory of God the Father.

Shining as Lights in the World

Therefore, my beloved, just as you have always obeyed me, not only in my presence, but much more now in my absence, work out your own salvation with fear and trembling; for it is God who is at work in you, enabling you both to will and to work for his good pleasure.

Do all things without murmuring and arguing, so that you may be blameless and innocent, children of God without blemish in the midst of a crooked and perverse generation, in which you shine like stars in the world. It is by your holding fast to the word of life that I can boast on the day of Christ that I did not run in vain or labour in vain. But even if I am being poured out as a libation over the sacrifice and the offering of your faith, I am glad and rejoice with all of you – and in the same way you also must be glad and rejoice with me.[40]

---

[40] Philippians 2:1-18.

It is worth noting that taking on the Son of God's mindset, where Christ emptied Himself of power, privilege and authority and became a servant, implied to Paul that the Christians at Philippi were to model their lives on the life of the servant king. The people of God were to 'shine like stars in the world'. In other words, the humble mind of Christ was to mould their lives and shine out of their faces to the surrounding pagan community. This is how we will display our own pictures of what God is like, among those around our Christian communities. Jesus exercised the power of love through service and sacrifice during His ministry. The Holy Spirit fills each believer with God's love, which is inherently self-sacrificial in nature, and which in turn enables us to serve others more selflessly.

The reign of the ascended Jesus, the Son of God, is a reign of love and service to the world, created by Father, Son and Holy Spirit. People cannot help but recognise that the God of the cross overcame sin and the dominion of the evil powers by love and sacrifice, when He is revealed to them by the Holy Spirit. Jesus did not wage a battle to destroy the forces of evil with weapons; rather, He conquered them by removing the power of sin and selfishness, which motivates the powers, by consuming it and overthrowing it through His once for all time sacrifice on Calvary's cross. God's reign is based on service, grace and forgiveness, not on manipulation, force and punishment. People can be attracted to a new picture of God by the cross of Christ, where God offers mercy and forgiveness to evil people and an evil world.

The cross displays the love of the Trinity for a selfish world by demonstrating that to be part of God's kingdom reign is to live unselfishly,nd sacrificially lovingly toward others, however warped their lives may be by sin. This is the picture of the heart of God that Christ's Spirit wants to display to the world through us, His followers. After all, the disciple becomes like his master. The Trinity had eternally planned, before the foundation of the world, that the Son of God would be sacrificed for the whole world.[41] In

---

[41] John 17:1-4.

other words, Father, Son and Holy Spirit have always been defined by sacrificial love that puts the other first. The picture of God portrayed by Christian communities needs to be expressed as love and grace towards a world that does not know what God is really like.

How will people form attachments to the family of God to which our communities belong?

Attachment to the family of God

It is my conviction that our Christian communities need to consider that they are connected to the Trinity's family: Father, Son and Holy Spirit. By extension, this also means that we need to be aware of the way psychology can help us to understand how human beings form attachments to their communities. Psychology informs us that we all obtain our basic working models of how to relate to others from our sense of belonging to our biological families, or from the care provided by our caregivers during childhood and adolescence. Families can enable children to view parents as trustworthy and deserving of their love. In my own upbringing, despite the faults and failings of my parents, I knew I was loved and that I could trust my parents to care for me. It was also a great encouragement to me that they remained together over the course of their lives.

No family is fully functional, but there is a basic minimum that is required if children are to successfully form meaningful attachments with others over a lifetime. This is obviously very important to how our Christian families, and our Christian communities, help us to become attached healthfully to others. Are our communities safe environments, where people are welcome to make mistakes and to learn from them without feeling that everything they do is under scrutiny, because of a judgemental mindset within our groups?

In functional families, where children feel free to explore the world and safe to develop their own working models of how to relate to others with empathy, it is important that their mistakes are treated as something perfectly normal if they are to learn from them.

Families are the first place we obtain our sense of belonging. It is hoped that parents who are reading this book now are seriously seeking to have the intimate abiding presence of Father, Son and Spirit at the centre of their family's lives. 'A family that prays together stays together' is not just an old Christian adage, in my view. Prayer is the language families use to come into the presence of God's family.

From a psychological perspective, it may be said that we obtain our basic working models of relating to others, whether that be God or people, from our early childhood experiences, based on our early relationships with our caregivers. According to the psychologist Bowlby, each of us constructs an internal working model (IWM) of how we can safely form attachments with others.[42] A person's IWM produces a personal representation of the child's (or our own)

---

[42] Collicutt, *The Psychology of Christian Character Formation*, p. 67.

world of social relationships. Joanna Collicutt suggests that others come to be viewed as 'more or less trustworthy, dependable, benevolent and accessible based on the child's experiences of the quality of care given to them in their early childhood'. She adds, 'It also represents [the child's] self in relation to others as deserving, lovable, of value, socially competent and so on.'[43]

These are obviously rather general comments regarding a child's development of IWM. What it is important to recognise is that this model helps us to understand how children, later adolescents, and still later adults, form attachments with others, which in the end will hopefully enable them to feel that they belong to others in mutual relationships. I would argue that God designed each of us to define our IWM based on the quality of relationships we encounter in our interactions with each other.

Collicutt also accepts that each of us obtains our own pictures of what we almost instinctively think and feel regarding what God is like. This begins in our earliest childhood experiences (once again), especially with our primary caregivers. She comments regarding our attachment to God:

> The undoubted connection between attachment and faith led Kirkpatrick to wonder if individual differences in our childhood attachment relationships might be expressed in adult life as individual differences in the way we relate to God. This question has given rise to an enormous body of research across the world that is still in progress. ... The findings are complex, but there seems to be reasonably good support for the theory that divine attachment can work in two ways: our relationship with God can correspond to the secure relationship we experienced with our primary caregivers or our relationship with God can compensate for the insecure relationship we experienced with our primary caregivers.[44]

---

[43] Collicutt, *The Psychology of Christian Character Formation*, p. 67.
[44] Collicutt, *The Psychology of Christian Character Formation*, p. 70.

This is vital to take on board as we consider how our Christian communities shape their members to relate to God. Moreover, the pictures of God that our communities portray will have direct bearing on the types of people who are attracted to them. For example, if our Christian community is made up of people who had positive attachment experiences with their caregivers, the people within it will have a faith that is 'likely to find in God a warmth, availability and intimacy that corresponds to what they enjoyed with [their] parents as they grew up'.[45] This in turn may attract those who did not form positive attachments, who grew up 'insecurely attached and who later came ... to an adult faith [who are] likely to find in God a warmth, availability and intimacy that compensates for what ... was denied by ... parents as [they] grew up.'[46] In this simple illustrative manner we can see how our communities are as much the by-product of our

Identity based on a shared image of God that welcomes anyone

Image of God Ministries

'Image of God exists to help draw men and women closer to God's will for their lives. Our focus is to provide tools that will enhance your life as you pursue what it means to be created in the image of God.'

Young adults are invited to attend their numerous conferences and concerts: 'Image of God's mission is to sponsor events that provide resources and tools that inspire our participants to integrate God's Word into their personal lives as they invest into their ministries.'

Some of their core values are: 'Imparting the message of hope and healing; intimate fellowship with one another; introducing others to Jesus Christ. Image of God shares with all men and women, regardless of their religious affiliation, the love, acceptance and completeness God has for us in him.'

http://www.imageofgod.org/about.htm

---

[45] Collicutt, *The Psychology of Christian Character Formation*, p. 70.
[46] Collicutt, *The Psychology of Christian Character Formation*, p. 70.

early attachments to our caregivers as they are a divine work of transformation.

A new desire for Generations Y and Z: spiritual fathers and mothers

An issue which is receiving growing recognition among a number of my colleagues is that young people are starting to seek spiritual fathers and mothers, as they have not found in their own families a spiritual role model for them to take into adult life. Our churches need to provide for these young adults an environment in which they can engage with those who have had some years of life experience in their own Christian journeys. Mature Christian men and women could help shape these young men's and women's own journeys, to help them find ways to attach more deeply and meaningfully with God and others.

Perhaps an important narrative that needs to inform the picture of God that our communities portray is that of God as *Abba* (Aramaic for 'Dad', or 'Daddy'), which framed Jesus' own way of addressing His Father. He taught His disciples, in the Lord's Prayer,[47] to address God as 'Father' (*Abba*). God as 'Dad' is a caregiver and life-shaping mentor, whom we can trust, as He is the all-loving Father of the cosmos who secures all peoples' futures to be good.

We are told by Paul in Romans 8 that we have received the spirit of the Son of God, who enables us to converse with the Father, as our *Abba*, on a spiritual wavelength of deep communion in our hearts.[48] It is the same Spirit, according to Paul in the same passage, who agrees with our spirits that we belong to *Abba*'s (Dad's) family.[49] In other words, we belong to the family in which Father, Son and Spirit are our divine caregivers. We relate to Jesus as brother (or sister) and Lord. We relate to the Father as Dad and

---

[47] Matthew 6:9.
[48] Romans 8:15.
[49] Romans 8:16.

mentor; we relate to the Spirit as the sensitive feminine s
that cares for, and further nurtures us, to become even mor
attached to *Abba*'s family. We belong to the family of the T
Our family identity is based on our participation in the life cycl
Trinity's family, expressed as togetherness, to which each of us i
sure we want to belong.[50]

Father, Son (Daughter) and Spirit need to be at the centre of our shared lives as Christian families and communities. The mission of the Trinity is for people to discover what their family is like, through the way our Christian communities live and breathe out God's presence, in behaviours that help people to trust the God with whom we fellowship together deeply. Part of God's identity, as a missionary, is that He seeks and finds lost and injured people in the midst of the dire situations they often find themselves inhabiting.

The communities where hurting and faith-seeking people live need to be the places where we live out our Christian lives. Our lives, practised in smaller, intentional Christian communities which meet in places such as homes, pubs and clubs, might be the first opportunities people have to encounter the God to whom we belong. Our Christian communities need to understand the impact of the way they portray God to others, by the ways that Christians behave towards one another. Are faith-seekers making contact with our communities viewing these encounters as positive or negative events in their lives? The one universal truth here is that our communities will be scrutinised for the kind of picture of God they portray. Too often we hear claims that Christians are hypocrites.

I think much of this language comes down to people having had bad experiences with those who profess to be disciples of Christ. It is hard to cultivate Christian communities that are open and intimate, welcoming and friendly, pleasant and generous, hospitable and supportive, because of the virus of individualism that too often has made church attendance another quick,

---

[50] Paul S. Fiddes, *Participating in God: A Pastoral Doctrine of the Trinity*, Louisville: Westminster John Knox Press (2000), pp. 12-13, 33-34, 37-39, 44-45, 51-55, 71-75.

luct, to be engaged with for an hour or two
rd for faith-seekers to discover God's love in
s type, because people leave quickly after
get on with their private lives. How might
isage the way they picture God to faith-
Christ's new commandment?

> 'I give you a new commandment, that you love one
> another. Just as I have loved you, you also should love one
> another. By this everyone will know that you are my
> disciples, if you have love for one another.'[51]

The reader may wish to reflect on this commandment in the light of Jesus' non-privatised life of sacrifice and service to the communities among which He walked.

All that I have communicated in this chapter is based on the primary conviction that the major way we come to know what God is like is through Christ's love lived out among His people as an ongoing incarnation of His presence by His communitarian self-giving Spirit. This commandment must always remain fresh and true to the atmospheres of our communities. This is costly, because it takes time – something we feel that we have too little of – to enable us to spend more time together in intentional fellowship. Jesus said to His disciples that to know Him was to know the Father.[52] The Greek word for 'to know' here speaks of knowledge that comes from friendships and trust-based relationships. This implies that our communities need to spend intentional time together in fellowship, outside of formal, structured worship gatherings. Hence the first place we obtain our picture of God is through the divine Son who reveals the Father:

---

[51] John 13:34-35.
[52] John 14:7.

'Those who love me will keep my word, and my Father will love them, and we will come to them and make our home with them.'[53]

This home is to be found with Trinity's presence at the heart of our interactions in our Christian communities, as well as in our broader missional interactions with secular society. Ultimately, it will include all of us being together in the eternal kingdom of God. The picture of God portrayed in our communities will need to literally be that *Abba* Father, the Spirit as our sensitive caring Mother, and Jesus as our Brother (Sister) are at home among us. Our times of fellowship need to overflow with Their presence. We all belong to the Trinity's family. This is what I term the mission of the Trinity (*missio Trinitatis*): it is a deeply meaningful prophetic gesture among our multicultural Christian communities, which need to be welcoming to those who are seeking to come home to *Abba*. *Missio Trinitatis* describes God's mission as to reconcile all peoples into Trinity's family. *Missio Dei* can imply a less intimate picture of God as a more transcendent unattached other. Hence I prefer the Trinitarian language.

Our communities need to portray a picture of *Abba*'s family values to all who gather together. Faith-seekers may find the one true God, who may be termed *Abba*, Mother, Brother and Sister among us, wherever we live out our lives in secular local communities. We need to visibly convey God our *Abba*, Mother, Brother and Sister in our places of work, leisure activities and homes, etc., because we are part of the mobile missional body of Christ,[54] sent out by the Trinity family to minister to the multicultural peoples that the Spirit of Christ is calling to come home to *Abba*'s family.

---

[53] John 14:23.
[54] 1 Corinthians 12.

Conclusions

In this chapter we have traced how our communities need to frame their identities with reference to the image of Christ. Our inner picture of Christ will inevitably shine out to others through our actions and words. Jesus came to reveal the heart of *Abba*, His beloved Father, to a lost world. Our Christian communities are part of the Trinity's family, built on sacrificial love where everyone can belong to God's eternal family. The mission of the Trinity is to welcome all peoples in our multicultural societies to become part of God's family, made up of all peoples. The picture of God portrayed by the quality of God's all-embracing love, lived out through the behaviours of people in our communities, will attract faith-seekers to the God who lives in our hearts and to whom we pour forth through words and deeds of love. The goal of Trinity-shaped community life is for all peoples to come to trust Father, Mother and Son (Daughter) so that the whole of society and all of its structures of government, education, health-care, business, etc. may be filled with the presence of the love of Trinity family and that all of its once lost participants belong to Trinity family.

Part 2

Biblical foundations to the contextualised picture of God as the Multicultural Trinity

Part 2

Biblical foundations to the contextualised picture of God as the Multicultural Trinity

Chapter 4
The mission of God and the multicultural Spirit of Jesus

The books of Luke and Acts may be said to offer casebook-like narratives of how *missio Trinitatis* or *missio Dei* take place in the real world of human life and history. Luke–Acts is not as such deeply invested with Trinitarian language, but it is strongly implied. How is a theology of *missio Trinitatis* (or *missio Dei*) supported in the New Testament? How can a theology of the MT be practically illustrated? What can we learn from the Luke–Acts case narratives about the way we can participate in the *missio Trinitatis*?

Among the documents that make up the New Testament, the books of Luke and Acts provide an interesting missional perspective on the ministry of Jesus. A. M. Hunter recognised the basic structure of the gospels and Acts, which are essentially framed around the articulation of the works and words of Jesus.[55] He portrayed Jesus' mission as a door-to-door battle with the forces of evil which are pitted against the kingdom of God, with the kingdom being established in the context of everyday life as a kind of guerrilla warfare led by Jesus.[56] In Luke–Acts, God's reign is pictured as coming through the doings and teachings of Jesus. This manifestation of the reign of God, in terms of the life of Jesus and through His Spirit after His ascension, was the decisive turning point in history, which will in the end lead to the universal

---

[55] A. M. Hunter, *The Work and Words of Jesus*, London: SCM Press (1973), chapters 1 and 2.
[56] Hunter, *The Work and Words of Jesus*, chapter 3.

eschatological[57] reign of God being finally established at the close of the age.[58] Eckhard Schnabel comments:

> Jesus' ministry defined a missionary ministry in the proper sense: he understood himself as 'sent' by God (Lk 4:43) to gather 'the lost sheep of the house of Israel' (Mt 15:24). Jesus traveled through Galilee, visiting villages and towns, proclaiming the good news of the dawn of God's kingdom, calling Israel to repent and to believe in the present fulfillment of God's covenant promises. Jesus saw himself as anointed by God's Spirit (Lk 4:18), who set off the liberating power of the turning point of God's history with his people and with the world through his teaching activity, through healing the sick and through liberating people from demons, this making visible the eschatological power of God (Mt 12:28-29). It was precisely in this sense that his message was euangelion, 'good news' (Mt 4:23; 11:5, following Is 61:1), the proclamation that God's kingdom had arrived (Mk 1:14-15; cf. Tg. Isa. 52:7). At the same time he gathered students to train them as 'fishers of people,' coworkers in his own missionary activity.[59]

This chapter will focus on the books of Luke and Acts. Luke's gospel covers the mission of Jesus, ending with the resurrected Lord instructing His disciples to wait in Jerusalem for the promise of the Father.[60] Acts sets out the continuing mission of Jesus through the Holy Spirit.[61] Undoubtedly the same writer produced Luke and Acts, as the basic language and structure of both books are very

---

[57] The end of the present world as we know it and the invasion of God's kingdom into every sphere of the world.

[58] Matthew 28:20.

[59] Eckhard J. Schnabel, *Early Christian Mission: Jesus and the Twelve*, Vol. 1, Downers Grove: IVP (2004), p. 207.

[60] Luke 24:49.

[61] Acts 1:1-4.

similar.[62] If we accept this as true, then Acts 1:1 provides an interesting insight into how Luke thought about the mission of Jesus:

> In the first book, O Theophilus, I have dealt with all that Jesus began to do and teach, until the day when he was taken up, after he had given commandment through the Holy Spirit to the apostles whom he had chosen.[63]

Luke begins the book of Acts by indicating that his first volume, the gospel, dealt with what 'Jesus began to do and teach'. The word 'began' comes from the Greek word *erxato*, in the past tense. This beginning of the words and works of Jesus, by implication, will continue as the stories of Acts unfold to the reader. The question is, how does Luke conceive of this continuing of the delivery of Jesus' ministry in human history? Probably the best clues are provided in Luke and Acts. The prologue to Acts continues to help our understanding as it speaks of Jesus:

> And while staying with them he charged them not to depart from Jerusalem, but to wait for the promise of the Father, which, he said, 'you heard from me, for John baptized with water, but before many days you shall be baptized with the Holy Spirit.'[64]

The 'promise' of the Lord is that the Father will send the Spirit. This has a definite Trinitarian ring to it. The coming of the Spirit was

---

[62] F. Scott Spencer, *Journeying through Acts: A Literary–Cultural Reading,* Peabody: Hendricksen Publishers (2004). Also see the book of essays edited by Jerome Neyrey for a good introduction to the social world of the books of Luke and Acts: Jerome H. Neyrey, (Ed.), *The Social World of Luke–Acts: Models for Interpretation,* Peabody: Hendricksen Publishers (2005).
[63] Acts 1:1-2, RSV.
[64] Acts 1:4-5, RSV.

to provide the motivating power for the disciples to engage in witnessing:

> 'You shall receive power when the Holy Spirit has come upon you; and you shall be my witnesses in Jerusalem and in all Judea and Samaria and to the end of the earth.'[65]

The pneumatology[66] of Acts is based on the concept of Christ's disciples participating with His Spirit in witnessing to the living Christ, who continues to do and teach through their missional testimonies and activities. *Missio Dei* is defined in Luke–Acts as the continuing work of Christ through His followers in the age of the Spirit of Jesus. Of course, it is important to note that we never find the words *missio Dei* used anywhere in the biblical literature. Peter's speech to the Jews on the day of Pentecost is in the context of the giving of the gift of tongues.[67] This gift is meant to support the early claim, made in the introduction to Acts, that Jesus' articulation of His words and deeds were a beginning, which assumes a continuance with the coming of the Spirit, through the agency of the apostles and disciples: they would be the ones who would act as the missional vehicles through which Christ would continue His mission. Peter declares to the crowd:

> 'This Jesus God raised up, and of that we all are witnesses. Being therefore exalted at the right hand of God, and having received from the Father the promise of the Holy Spirit, he has poured out this which you see and hear.'[68]

Peter's kerygmatic (proclamation) speech is in actuality conceived of as the continuing witness of Jesus, which is now interpreted through His apostles, who have His Spirit motivating them to utter His words to the early messianic community. It is also

---

[65] Acts 1:8, RSV.
[66] The study of how we understand the work of the Holy Spirit.
[67] Acts 2:1-5.
[68] Acts 2:32-33, RSV.

important to remember that the apostles taught and did miraculous signs as part of their witness for Christ in participation with the Spirit.[69] The living Jesus is actively pictured in the words and deeds of the apostles because He is alive and working through them as His vehicles of missional ministry. Peter's message was motivated by the presence of the Spirit through the sign of glossolalia.[70] Glossolalia seemed to be a Spirit-given ability, enabling the apostles to speak in languages they had not previously known, and endowing Peter with the ability to deliver what the Spirit wanted conveyed to His audience on the day of Pentecost.[71] The new believers after Pentecost:

> devoted themselves to the apostles' teaching and fellowship, to the breaking of bread and the prayers. ...
> And fear came upon every soul; and many wonders and signs were done through the apostles.'[72]

It was not just the first apostles and disciples who were to receive the missional gift of communicating and interpreting the gospel by glossolalia; it was also to be part of every succeeding believer's experience of God, if we take the testimony of Acts seriously. Meaningful and accurate interpretation of the first-century culture-bound language found in the New Testament and Acts is provided to believers so that they can interpret these same Scriptures in a way that is suited to contemporary cultural contexts. Peter called the new believers to repent, and upon doing so they too would be invested with the presence of the Spirit:

> 'Repent, and be baptized every one of you in the name of Jesus Christ for the forgiveness of your sins; and you shall receive the gift of the Holy Spirit. For the promise is to you

---

[69] Acts 2.
[70] Acts 2:1-5.
[71] Acts 2:14-23.
[72] Acts 2:42-43, RSV.

and to your children and to all that are far off, every one whom the Lord our God calls to him.'[73]

The promise of the *missio pneuma* ('mission of the Spirit') is not limited to the Christian church of the first century; it is also a promise 'to your children and to all that are far off'. *Missio Dei*, by its very nature, is based on the *missio Christi* ('mission of Christ'), as well as the *missio pneuma*, in the terms set out in the theology of Luke–Acts. Acts' missiology is *pneuma-Christic* (based on the work of the Spirit of Christ). This can be witnessed in the later theological compass of the book. But we must remember that the coming of the Spirit is said to be a gift from the Father through the risen Christ. The picture of God portrayed in Acts is of the living Spirit of Jesus who is felt and seen to be phenomenologically present in the words and deeds of His followers. What they do and say bears the stamp of what Jesus said and did in Luke's account.

This is further seen in Paul's ministry. When Paul was travelling through ancient Asia Minor, he and his team are said to have been guided by the Holy Spirit:

> And they went through the region of Phrygia and Galatia, having been forbidden by the Holy Spirit to speak the word in Asia. And when they had come opposite Mysia, they attempted to go into Bithynia, but the Spirit of Jesus did not allow them; so, passing by Mysia, they went down to Troas. And a vision appeared to Paul in the night: a man of Macedonia was standing beseeching him and saying, 'Come over to Macedonia and help us.' And when he had seen the vision, immediately we sought to go on into Macedonia, concluding that God had called us to preach the gospel to them.[74]

It may have struck the astute reader that there are two ways the Holy Spirit is spoken of in this passage: 'Holy Spirit' and 'Spirit of

---

[73] Acts 2:38-39, RSV.
[74] Acts 16:6-10, RSV.

80

Jesus'. Luke brings both phrases together, which would imply that he used them synonymously. The further implication is that the work of the Holy Spirit is identified with Jesus' mission. Just as Jesus was sent on the mission, which Luke 4:18 and 43 imply, so the Spirit continues that work as the 'Spirit of Jesus' through His missional people. The *missio pneuma* and the *missio Christi* are conflated. The Spirit that is now guiding apostles and disciples, in terms of the *missio Dei*, is Jesus' Spirit. The Spirit of Jesus enables the multicultural people of God to rightly understand and interpret the Scriptures in the context of the new horizons of different contemporary cultural contexts. The living Jesus is actively portrayed in the ministry of all Christians who are motivated to participate in the mission of Jesus as His followers. Their lives bear the stamp and hallmark of the Jesus revealed in Luke's gospel, who acts as our benchmark to measure the work of the Spirit of Jesus in our lives. People who do not as yet know Jesus will come to know Him on a phenomenological level as they experience His continued presence through the words and works of His missional ministers. The picture of God portrayed in Luke–Acts is a phenomenological experience: people encounter Jesus through His continuing presence, works and actions that can be witnessed as authentic manifestations of His presence in His followers' lives. The Spirit of Jesus interprets the messages revealed through the Scriptures to new peoples so that they can directly be anointed to intelligently apply them suited to their own cultural contexts.

The Spirit of Jesus continues the words and works of Jesus alongside and through the apostolic Christian community. Did Luke understand this in binatarian terms (as a joined work of two people or forces), where the Son and the Spirit work together independently of the heavenly Father? Part of the answer to this question is to be found in Acts 1:4, where Christ is claimed to have said that the Holy Spirit's coming at Pentecost was based on the 'promise of the Father'. The Father is also at work in terms of *missio Trinitatis*. The Trinity community is drawing all fractured communities of the world to identify the new kingdom life and community portrayed through the people of Christ – His mobile missional body actively present among them in the world.

This 'promise' orientates Acts' portrayal of *missio Dei* to include all three persons of the Trinity. Of course, Luke–Acts is not explicit in terms of a Trinitarian theology. It has long been recognised by theologians that it is quite unadvisable to try to construct systematic theology based on accounts that were framed to be narratives. Narratives, like those in Acts, function in different ways from the way Paul uses theological language in his letters, for example. Having made this claim, some scholars, such as N. T. Wright, have not been slow in reminding us that what at first seems to be dense argument in Paul is actually based on Paul's Jewish background, where behind the mention of names like Abraham he assumes that early Jewish messianic Christians will remember the whole story.[75] In other words, they would have understood much more readily what Paul was writing simply because their whole theological worldview was broadened and brought to life by reliving the stories of their forefathers which informed their present stories. They could imagine themselves in the stories of Abraham's life and journeys as if these were part of their own journeys.

The Father, Christ and Holy Spirit are all

> **Identity based on an emerging picture that God is shaping a community to become!**
>
> Mosaic Church, which meets in three locations in London
>
> 'Mosaics are made up of tiny, broken bits of stone that are different colours, shapes and sizes. They are then pieced together to form a picture that none of the stones could express on their own.
>
> 'We are convinced that this is what the church should be like. Mosaic draws lots of different people together into a family that's on a mission. And hopefully, by the way we love Jesus, invest in each other, give to the needy, and seek the best for the city of Leeds and the nations, you will see a beautiful picture of God forming.'
>
> http://mosaic-church.org.uk/about/vision-values

---

[75] N. T. Wright, *Paul: Fresh Perspectives*, London: SPCK (2005).

identifiable in the Luke–Acts worldview, albeit not in systematic theological terms. I would say the picture of God that we find in Luke–Acts is that of the missional Christian community directly seeking to participate in the ongoing work of the Spirit of Jesus. Hence the identities of our missional churches probably need to be conveyed to faith-seekers in terms of the living Jesus, reaching out to them through His Spirit-sensitive followers. I believe that this interpretation of the Jesus of Luke–Acts needs to form the bedrock of our missional church life and activities among faith-seekers. Indeed, we have traced some evidence for this in what we have discussed so far in this chapter. However, it is not as such the aim of this chapter to build a case for the Trinity in our consideration of the book of Acts, or the gospel of Luke, for that matter. But we must note that the picture of God, where the Trinity invites new people into its multicultural family, is seemingly fundamental to the big picture of God's mission in the New Testament documents in general, and Luke-Acts does not undermine that thesis.

More importantly, *missio Dei* theology is more than simply suggested by both books, which were written by the same author. The mission of God is set in the context of the mission of Jesus in the gospel, and is continued in Acts by the mission of the Spirit of Jesus. Luke–Acts helps to make the case for a Spirit-centred missiology for the missional church, which portrays God to faith-seekers as actively looking to draw them into the Trinitarian family. The way the early church engaged in *missio Dei*, in the nascent community, was by the apostles and disciples having received the Spirit, as well as the community being enabled to discern the Spirit's voice, as She guided them to engage with Christ's continuing mission ahead of the church. Acts' missiology portrays an experiential feeling of Christ's continuing presence and ministry. For example, we noted how Paul experienced the influence of the Spirit of Jesus, who guided his mission team to go to Macedonia. It must also be noted that Acts reminds us that it was the Lord who continued to add daily to 'those who were being saved' as part of the early church in Jerusalem.[76]

Acts sets out a spiritual and missional theology as central to the church's participation in the mission of Jesus, where the Spirit guided the disciples to where they needed to take the gospel next. Spiritual guidance sets the work of the *missio pneuma* to be the compass of where missional engagement is to take place among multicultural people groups who as yet do not know the living Christ. Acts shows how faith-seekers had encounters with the still active, living Jesus, which brought to life the reality of the picture of Christ that Christian evangelists shared with them. The picture of God, conveyed in the terms of Acts Christianity, is of a real living being, Jesus Christ, who is much more than a fanciful story that Christians told. Our missional communities today need not just to convey the picture of Christ to seekers, but also to be environments where the living Jesus is actually encountered.

Moreover, the words of the living Jesus need to inhabit the believer's mind, so that the Spirit can bring those words to life when they are communicated to people who do not as yet know Christ. The gift of glossolalia to the first believers was not just to enable them to remember Jesus' sayings or parables, but it also enabled Peter to interpret the meaning of Jesus' words and works in a way that was appropriate to the context of his Jewish audience. We need the Spirit's help to interpret Jesus in a relevant, meaningful way to faith-seekers.

The hidden mystery of Christ revealed to and through missional communities

This insight is vital in terms of the study of ancient biblical apocalyptic prophecy, which came to take on what is known as Raz Pesher interpretation. Daniel 2 is often used to illustrate this. A good way of understanding how Raz Pesher works is to say that it was not enough for a prophet to receive a message from Yahweh,

---

[76] Acts 2:47, RSV.

but they also needed to obtain the interpretation from God concerning how it applied to His people. Luke–Acts uses Raz Pesher hermeneutics, so it is important to obtain a thumbnail sketch of how this approach to understanding the revelation of Christ to the world works. Raz Pesher interpretation has to do with the very nature of an imminent hermeneutic, where God is about to act in human history. It means that a mysterious message or vision, which is not as yet understood by the recipient (the Raz – ie the mystery), has to be made sense of by the Pesher (interpretation), to unveil the mystery. The term 'apocalyptic' describes the uncovering, or unveiling, of a mystery.[77] The mystery needs interpreting, and the Spirit of prophecy is the means by which the mystery is decoded, or interpreted, suited to the context of the group with whom we want to share the good news of Jesus.

This is the kind of idea behind the gift of glossolalia in Acts: the mysterious language of God was enacted in the sending of Jesus, who died for our sins, rose again and then returned to His Father in Heaven. This mystery is interpreted with the help of the Spirit of Jesus by God's people today, just as the Spirit enabled Peter to interpret the mysterious pre-planned mission of God to reconcile the world through Christ, to his audience, suited to their context.[78]

Raz Pesher interpretation has a 'this is that' precision to it, in the sense that what has been a mystery is now specifically revealed and applied to the present context in which the people of God find themselves. In terms of presenting a picture of Christ to faith-seeking communities in our localities, we need the Spirit of Jesus to help us interpret the culture and then to frame the message so that it makes sense to them. In other words, mystery works in two directions: firstly, a new people group we want to work with has a culture that is somewhat mysterious to us; and secondly, our culture will be mysterious in some ways to them. The Spirit helps both sides to interpret what is mysterious to each about the other,

---

[77] Richard N. Longenecker, *Biblical Exegesis in the Apostolic Period,* Grand Rapids: Eerdmans (1999), pp. 24-27.
[78] Acts 2:38-39.

and Christ will be at the centre of the missional conversations we share, as the unseen guest who builds a hermeneutical bridge of shared understanding.

In terms of Peter's speech on the day of Pentecost, the mysterious Raz of the dying and risen Lord is applied to mean the specific fulfilment of God's plan to establish the kingdom of God for Israel and the nations of the world. The long-awaited inauguration of the restoration of Israel, so deeply desired in the first century as part of Second Temple Judaism, finds Peter enabled by the Spirit to interpret the meaning of the Jesus event to the specific context of his Jewish audience. By implication, this is what needs to happen in the way missional communities seek to communicate the meaning of Jesus to local people. Without the missional Raz Pesher being glossolalically discerned by those who seek to communicate the living Jesus to a new context, there will arguably be a deficiency in terms of understanding how Christ can transform that community.

Furthermore, research into a community to be reached for Christ requires that strategic planning for missional endeavours is based on the spiritual enlightenment which comes from the hermeneutic of Raz Pesher discernment. In other words, the Holy Spirit reveals to a Christian group who are to share the gospel with a new group that as yet has not been transformed by Christ the mystery of God's plans for that community. According to the epistle to the Ephesians, the gospel itself was a hidden mystery (a Raz) before it was disclosed (Pesher) to the world through Christ:

> To me, though I am the very least of all the saints, this grace was given, to preach to the Gentiles the unsearchable riches of Christ, and to make all men see what is the plan of the mystery hidden for ages in God who created all things; that through the church the manifold wisdom of God might now be made known to the principalities and powers in the heavenly places.[79]

---

[79] Ephesians 3:8-10, RSV.

Notice how the writer to the Ephesians also includes the 'church' as participating in the continuing disclosure of the revealed mystery of the gospel of Christ to the 'powers'. The powers can be local government organisations in a community, law enforcement, big businesses, and so on. The mystery of Christ's missional plans continues to be uncovered as missional communities continue to participate with the Spirit of Jesus in His ministry to reconcile people to God in their localities. The stories our communities convey about Christ, through their beliefs and practices, will portray a picture of God to faith-seekers that enables them to understand what was once shrouded in mystery for them, because Christ had not been effectively pictured to them through God's people. The ultimate goal of *missio Dei* is that all things will be finally unified with God in Christ, as the goal of salvation history.[80] This goal, of the full and final establishment of the kingdom of God as the *telos* (end) of history, will also need to provide those who become followers of Christ with the hope of peace in the eschatological kingdom.[81]

Geographic expansion of *missio Dei*

When the persecuted Christians went to Antioch following the martyrdom of Stephen,[82] Antioch became a new staging post for the missional activity of the messianic community, somewhat like Jerusalem had been at first.[83] The Antioch church sent Paul and Barnabas on their first missionary tour to the lower southern regions of Asia Minor. The church there became well enough established so that local prophets received the Spirit's instructions that these two men should be set apart for apostolic mission. It is vital that prophetic leaders follow prophetic intuitions, in order to

---

80 Ephesians 1:9-10.
81 Revelation 21:1-5.
82 Acts 8.
83 Acts 13:1-3.

discern what God is doing in their communities.[84] This may be thought of as missional propulsion similar to the early church's experiences, which were instigated by the Spirit to take the gospel to the multicultural peoples of the Greco–Roman Empire. The picture of Christ portrayed in Paul's ministry was based on the Christian heritage of Christ the inheritor of the multinational promises made to Abraham that would lead to all nations being blessed by salvation. The picture of God strongly implied in Acts is of the God who makes all nations part of the Lord's one family.

It is important to consider the commissioning of Paul and Barnabas in Antioch for their missionary work. The missionary tour that followed has become known as the first missionary journey:

> Now in the church at Antioch there were prophets and teachers, Barnabas, Simeon who was called Niger, Lucius of Cyrene, Manaen a member of the court of Herod the tetrarch, and Saul. While they were worshiping the Lord

---

[84] Donal Dorr, *Spirituality of Leadership: Inspiration, Empowerment, Intuition and Discernment*, Dublin: The Columba Press, (2006), pp. 123-133.

and fasting, the Holy Spirit said, 'Set apart for me
Barnabas and Saul for the work to which I have called
them.' Then after fasting and praying they laid their hands
on them and sent them off. ...
So, being sent out by the Holy Spirit, they went down to
Seleucia; and from there they sailed to Cyprus.[85]

It is important to note that the Spirit sets the duo apart, then the
prophets send them off on the mission that Christ has called them
to undertake. Just as Jesus was sent by the Father on a mission to
make God's love known to the world, so the Spirit of Jesus sends
these men on the same mission to make God known to the nations.
The strategy of the Antioch missional community is inspired by the
Holy Spirit. The Spirit led the prophets to communicate this
strategy to Paul and Barnabas.

It is vital that prophets help contemporary missional teams to
discover God's strategy for their local communities. The picture of
God in Acts is of the missionary Spirit of Jesus guiding His
missional people to follow Him as he continues His ministry
through them. The centrifugal missiology of Acts is propulsive in
nature, as movement remains at the very core of its defining
architecture. The ongoing mission of the Spirit of Jesus requires His
followers to see themselves as full-time committed missionaries
who take Christ into every part of their lives, 24 hours a day, seven
days a week.

Outward spirations of God's mission to multicultural society

The establishment of a new central hub, from which mission may
spiral (spirate) towards multicultural people groups in our Western
context, has at its heart practical spiritual discernment of what God
has called His people to do. The nature of *missio Dei* is defined by
Luke–Acts to be dynamic. Change comes when the Spirit of Jesus is
spiritually discerned by missional disciples who are determined to

---

[85] Acts 13:1-4, RSV.

follow in His footsteps. The missional church is not a static entity but a dynamic, purpose-driven, 'sending' community. Change will keep occurring in communities where the Spirit of Christ continues to guide the community on the *missio Dei*. The apostles and the other disciples were defined by being followers of Christ. The picture of God owned by modern-day disciples needs to be based on them seeing themselves as followers of the living Jesus and on the guidance of His Spirit. We need followers in missional communities today who can hear the voice of the Spirit of Christ.

The picture of the missional prophetic people of Christ

James Dunn has helped us understand that the Spirit's presence in the early church 'was most characteristically a divine power manifesting itself in inspired utterance'.[86] Some key texts that emphasise this are Acts 1:16; 3:18; 4:25; 28:25. The theologian Karkkainen follows Dunn's insight by declaring that 'this evidence fulfils Moses' desire that all the Lord's people would be prophets and that the Lord would put his Spirit upon them (Num. 11:29)'.[87] Peter's speech in Acts 2:14-21 sets out the conviction that God's people in general would receive the Spirit, and that the Spirit of prophecy was for young and old alike. The God of the prophets was at work among His people, who saw themselves as inspired by God's missional Spirit.

Acts 2 suggests that all believers would become endued, at a basic level at least, with the Spirit of prophecy. It is important to note that the quotation from Joel in Acts 2:14-21 has Christ's presence residing in God's sons and daughters. In other words, Acts encourages us to share more than a picture of Christ to those with whom we share His story; we also need to declare with certainty that this Jesus, on whom we model our lives, will reveal Himself to

---

[86] James D. Dunn, *Jesus and the Spirit,* London: SCM Press (1970), p. 699.
[87] Veli-Matti Karkkainen, *Pneumatology: The Holy Spirit in Ecumenical, International, and Contextual Perspective*, Grand Rapids: Baker Academic (2002), p. 31.

be alive to those who ask Him to do so. Acts 2 declares that all who call on the name of the Lord will be saved.

This kind of language is probably descriptive of the pneumatic closeness of the Spirit of the Lord Jesus to all who heard the gospel. Acts conceives of the missional Spirit of Jesus being close to those who are being confronted with the gospel. The story of the conversion of the Gentile Cornelius in Acts 10 demonstrates that Christ's Spirit was close at hand. Cornelius and his household were filled with the Spirit and spoke in tongues as a sign of their conversion.[88] The implication is that the Lord may be said to be a close intimate presence to those who call on His name.

Real encounters with the living Christ

Central to the theology of Acts is that the Spirit continues the mission of Jesus with the eschatological goal of the kingdom of God being finally realised. Peter's speech at Pentecost emphasised the need for the house of Israel to accept that God had 'made' Jesus 'both Lord and Christ.'[89] Those who repented on the day of Pentecost for their rebellion against the Lord's Christ by crucifying Him are said to have been 'cut to the heart'.[90] The living Jesus portrayed in Peter's speech made these Jewish people aware of His presence as He convicted them of their sin and rebellion. The response required of them was to be the same as for all who would follow after them:

> 'Repent, and be baptized every one of you in the name of Jesus Christ for the forgiveness of your sins; and you shall receive the gift of the Holy Spirit. For the promise is to you and to your children and to all that are far off, every one whom the Lord our God calls to him.'[91]

---

[88] Acts 10:44-46.
[89] Acts 2:36, RSV.
[90] Acts 2:37, RSV.
[91] Acts 2:38-39, RSV.

To be baptised 'in the name of Jesus Christ' equates with the earlier reference in Peter's speech that 'everyone who calls on the name of the Lord will be saved'.[92] This calling on the 'name of the Lord' required new followers of Christ to be subject to the Lord, and to put their trust in the Lord's Christ.[93] It would also require them to faithfully follow Him and to be obedient to Him as God's anointed King. It is on the basis of this kind of obedient faith that believers will seek the guidance of the Spirit of Jesus, that they may properly be claimed to be engaging in *missio Trinitatis*.

If we are to follow the guidance of the sovereign Spirit of Christ, as Newbigin suggested,[94] we have to seriously seek after God's prophetic Spirit to guide us in the discovery of God's mission towards our local communities. Newbigin called for the future of missiology in the West to evoke the prophetic voice to become manifest among God's people.

The ministry of Christ through those who equip God's people for *missio Trinitatis*

This prophetic missiology takes the revelation of God seriously. The God who reveals Himself does so as Father, Son and Holy Spirit. Therefore, when the church seeks to discern the missional guidance of the Spirit of Jesus, its apostolic ministry teams need to be fully engaged in seeking where their missional and evangelistic efforts are to be concentrated next. Ephesians 4:11-13 highlights what some have called the fivefold ministries, which consist of five key missional ministry roles to equip God's people to fully engage in God's mission:

> And his gifts were that some should be apostles, some prophets, some evangelists, some pastors and teachers, to equip the saints for the work of ministry, for building up

---

[92] Acts 2:21.

[93] Acts 2:36-39.

[94] Lesslie Newbigin, *The Open Secret: An Introduction to the Theology of Mission*, London: SPCK (1995), chapters 4 and 5.

> the body of Christ, until we all attain to the unity of the
> faith and of the knowledge of the Son of God, to mature
> manhood, to the measure of the stature of the fulness of
> Christ.[95]

These five gifts are needed to bring the church of Christ to full maturity. It is impossible to speak of the prophetic gift of missional ministry alone: we need to include all five. It will become clear by the end of this section why this is important. There is, of course, a spread of these gifts in the church of Christ, but too often the first three gifts are marginalised in many Christian denominations and networks. Hence apostles, prophets and evangelists are not welcome in many traditional denominations and networks.

Apostles tend to seek the new things of God, entrepreneurially beginning numerous new initiatives. Church planters often have an apostolic calling. They will be ahead of established congregations in setting up new initiatives, which can make established local churches both suspicious of and resistant to what their motives might be. The prophetic voice can also be marginalised; it will often be found alongside the kinds of leaders who are church planters. The prophetic gift tends to engage with the Spirit in the new things God is doing in a community, and it is a vital source for the apostolic planting team to listen to. Evangelists can also be a challenge to churches. They most often have great passion to share the good news they have of the Saviour with those who do not know Him as yet. The apostolic gift often goes hand in hand with the evangelistic gift.

Christian communities can go through a life cycle, starting at an entrepreneurial stage when they are first planted, moving to a growth stage where they seek to increase their numbers, then to a consolidation phase where they seek to establish structures that will sustain the community for the long haul, on to a more mature established stage where there are accepted beliefs and practices that define them, and finally to an aging stage where things become

---

[95] Ephesians 4:11-13, RSV.

fixed by received traditions that have become the defining beliefs. In the aging stage, communities can become inflexible and tend to exclude the gifts brought by apostles, prophets and evangelists, as they rock the proverbial boat of the aging community.

When this fixed stage defines a Christian community and becomes the norm, it is almost impossible for the gifts of apostle, prophet and evangelist to be part of the leadership structure. This is because the fixed stage focuses on maintaining the status quo. Pastors and teachers are needed in these cases. The best way to operate the church of Christ is for all five ministries to be part of the leadership team, or network in a network of churches.

It is notable that most Bible colleges are popping out pastors and teachers rather than apostles, prophets and evangelists. We need to equip future missional ministers who represent all five.

When the picture of God becomes the property of the church rather than the property of the living Jesus

It is possible for an aging established Christian group to make Christ its property, and to thus ensure that the living Jesus of mission is structurally excluded from the faith community. In other words, the picture of God portrayed by an inflexible aging community is of God caring for the dying. Having said this, this fixated stage of ecclesial development does not necessarily lose concern for the church to grow and for the gospel to be communicated to others. Yet this desire can be dampened by the need to keep the group stable. The question then becomes, 'How can we bring new blood into the church without upsetting the stability that members value?' Mostly this strategy fails, because when new people come with fresh ideas they soon become marginalised as established members want to keep things the same.

We noted above that church leadership structures in these kinds of Christian communities will often tend to be dominated by the pastoring and teaching gifts. As Frost and Hirsch have suggested, the pastor tends to be a 'humanizer' who wants to care for those for whom they are already responsible. The teacher can be a 'systematizer', valuing set structures in order to keep the congregation stable. These two gifts can become the controlling narrative that guide aging groups to resist change and change agents. At the same time, the pastors and teachers (usually in local churches a combination of the paid minister, paid teachers, elders and/or deacons) realise that things need to change or their churches will decline and enter a terminal phase – a situation which many smaller churches in the UK are now facing.[96] Hence, as Roxburgh suggests, leaders of this type are on the liminal edge.[97] How can they have the best of both worlds? How can they see growth without upsetting the apple cart and bruising the established apples? It is inevitable that the entry of apostolic, prophetic or evangelistic missional ministers into churches will lead to a certain amount of disruption and bruising. Yet these three gifts are also vital to have as part of the missional church, or alongside it, in order for the church to continue to emerge and connect with the missionary work of the sovereign Spirit of Christ. We can see all five gifts at work in the Luke–Acts narratives.[98]

What is implied by this discussion is that church structures need to exist which will, on the one hand, keep the people of God looking ahead centrifugally for the Spirit to continue guiding them to establish new missional communities. In other words, the church needs the first three leadership gifts. On the other hand, it also needs the gifts of pastors and teachers who establish and settle people into a relationship with Jesus Christ centripetally.

To put it another way, the church needs to look deeply towards the centre of the lives of those who are being formed into mature

---

[96] Michael Frost and Alan Hirsch, *The Shaping of Things to Come: Innovation and Mission For the 21st Century Church*, Australia: Baker Publishing Group (2013), Chapters 3-6.

[97] Alan J. Roxburgh, *The Sky is Falling !?! Leaders Lost in Transition*, Colorado: ACI Publishing (2005), pp. 78-99.

[98] Peter acted as a prophet and teacher – see Acts 2; Paul and Barnabas acted as evangelists – see Acts 13–14; Stephen acted as a deacon, teacher and pastor – see Acts 6–7.

disciples of Christ, as well as outwardly towards those who need, first of all, to become followers of Jesus. If the more mature followers of Jesus are strengthened in their spiritual connection to the Christ of self-revelation, they will be able to help new disciples to become like the Christ they follow. Hence discipleship structures that call established believers to become deeply grounded in Christ will also need to focus their attention away from the centre, outwards towards those with whom the missional Spirit is calling them to engage in order to shape yet more disciples.

The prophet, as missional leader, is the spiritual detective of the missional church. The picture of God as a missionary in the book of Acts challenges us to recognise Him as one who welcomes all peoples and cultures into His kingdom. I believe that the book of Acts helps us to formulate our theology to include the picture of God as the MT because the Trinity created the multicultural DNA of humankind to be part of the *imago Trinitatis* we all share. Acts demonstrates how the MT welcomed Greco–Roman multicultural people groups into God's missional family. Hence we are sent as the missional people of God to equip all people groups and cultures to be united as the one family of the MT.

God's people are called to participate in the ongoing work of the mission of the Spirit of Jesus. Jesus sends His people to complete His mission to reconcile and unite all peoples by God's love to live together as part of the MT's family. It is only as we set the prophetic gift in the context of the fivefold missional ministry structures of the local and universal church that we can understand that its primary function is to enable the people of God to keep connecting deeply with the voice of God. We need to keep on doing this so that disciples may continue to grow in Christ, and new disciples will become part of the MT's family.

The prophet may also be an apostle; the apostle Paul seemed to have both gifts, and he certainly was an evangelist, pastor and teacher as well. He was multi-gifted. However, the apostle and prophet do not always have the gift of evangelising and bringing new people to a saving faith. Not everyone is as extraordinary as Paul was in this regard. Hence evangelists are needed.

Conclusion

Our discussions in this chapter point to what we all need to recognise: that *missio Trinitatis* theology needs to be discovered through the prophetic guidance of the Spirit of Jesus. The Spirit draws the attention of the church to the model life of Jesus, the representative human being. Jesus is the model disciple who connects us through His divine–human nature with the Trinity's family. Jesus is the *imago Dei* upon which we all frame our identities, with reference to His life and teachings. The persons of God revealed as Father, Son and Holy Spirit are meant to be understood as a representation of the perfect functional divine family. Therefore, in John's writings particularly, all followers are children of God – God's sons and daughters in God's family.[99]

The topic of the next chapter will be John's missional community, and will link the Luke–Acts theology of Jesus the representative divine–human with the implied Johannine theology of the Trinity, consisting of Father, Son and Spirit.

---

[99] John 1:13; 1 John 5:1-2.

Chapter 5
John's missional community

To what extent can we speak of the churches that John oversaw as missional communities? Did they have a picture of God which made them missional? This is an important question asked by literary critics of the gospel that has helped scholars to address its core themes. Literary and historical criticism seeks to understand the work of an author in terms of their influence on its worldview and outlook. The author puts their own interpretations on the significance of events in the way they structure their material, and in the way they portray the lives of key figures to the communities for whom they write. More recently, the introduction of narrative criticism has helped biblical scholars to obtain a deeper understanding of how the narrative frameworks of ancient literature, like John's gospel, convey a storied worldview. In the first instance, the storied worldview of the author is represented in how the various sayings, stories and parables have been structured. The question about John's gospel is, 'For what kind of community did the writer frame his Jesus stories?' There have been a number of creative suggestions. We will turn our attention to these soon.

The particular picture of God portrayed in John's gospel focuses on the heavenly Father. Jesus says to one of His disciples that to know Him is to know the Father.[100] This means that knowing what Christ is like enables the disciples to know what the Father is like. The all-time favourite passage, which is often quoted by evangelical Christians, is taken from John 3:16-17:

---

[100] John 14:8-9.

'For God so loved the world that he gave his only Son, so that everyone who believes in him may not perish but may have eternal life. Indeed, God did not send the Son into the world to condemn the world, but in order that the world might be saved through him.'

John's emphasis on the Son having been given to the world is very important, as it directly implies that Father and Son belong to humanity as much as humanity belongs to Them.

The terms 'Father' and 'Son' are family language, and also mean that the Father has those who trust in Christ as His sons and daughters. The picture of God in John's gospel is that of the family of God, to which John's gospel communities belonged.

The theologian Michael Moynagh discusses approaches to creating gospel communities and offers an important contribution to those who want to frame their identities around the good news about Christ.[101] Indeed, Father, Son and Holy Spirit make up the three persons of the one God, as implied in this gospel, after all God is called Spirit in this gospel.[102] This means believers have a picture of God where God and His people belong together as part of His eternal family. God loves us and gives us eternal life as a present-day possession.[103] Hence we are eternally secure in His family. God is active among His people, and through them among the world of non-believers, so that the whole world might become part of the Father's family if they come to know Him through the revelation of the Father in Christ.

I remember one young women who joined a Christian community I led. Barbara (not her real name) had come from an abusive family background. She had never really known unconditional love, or the experience of feeling secure. As she came to understand that the heavenly Father loved her for who she was,

---

[101] Michael Moynagh, *Being Church, Doing Life: Creating Gospel Communities Where Life Happens,* Oxford: Monarch Books (2014).
[102] John 4:22-24.
[103] John 5:24-25.

her confidence grew and she was able to develop strong friendships with some of the people in our Christian community.

This is one example of how a Christian group can provide an experience of belonging to the Trinity's family, by modelling a picture of God through their behaviours that welcomes new people, providing them with secure, trust-based friendships on which they can build to become an integral part of God's family.

Identity based on a purposeful picture of God

Life Church – Cuffley and Potters Bar (UK)

'Purpose Driven Churches Changing lives on Purpose: The purpose of our church is summarised in a single sentence based on two key scriptures:

"To Grow by Living Out the Great Commandment and the Great Commission."

'The Great Commandment: "Jesus said, 'Love the Lord your God with all your heart... soul... and mind. This is the first and greatest commandment. And the second is like it: Love your neighbour as yourself. All the Law and the Prophets hang on these two commandments."'

'The Great Commission: "Jesus said, 'Go and make disciples of all nations, baptising them in the name of the Father and of the Son and of the Holy Spirit, and teaching them to obey everything I have commanded you."'

http://www.lifechurch.uk.com/life-church-about-us/

Applying the implied Trinitarian theology of John to our contexts

It is important to obtain a better understanding of how the implied Trinitarian theology of the gospel of John can be applied to our own missional communities and their varying contexts. To achieve this, we need to understand something of how John framed his gospel for his community's context.

John's gospel is framed around the purpose of the Father in sending the Son to reveal what the Father is like to humanity.[104] It will be useful to trace clues that come from both the gospel and the first letter of John, as they belong together, in my estimation. It has been suggested that the letter and the gospel were not written in close proximity to each other, but this does not undermine the very close relationship between the literary style and themes of both. Moreover, there is a broad scholarly appreciation that the same Christian community was being addressed in both.[105]

What have Johannine scholars had to say about the kind of community for which the gospel was written?

Views of the Johannine community

The theologian Larry Hurtado believes that the Johannine Christian community consisted of Jewish Christian believers who were Hellenists (they spoke Greek and were influenced by Hellenistic culture).[106] After the destruction of the temple in Jerusalem in AD 70 by Titus Vespasian's son, these Christians had moved to the North, to Galilee, with other Jews from Judea. They still probably had some affiliations with the Jewish synagogues and with those who were still broadly sympathetic to the Jesus movement. Hurtado argues that there was a decisive conflict and break with the Jewish community at a point in time, probably in the 90s, which meant that John's Christian group split off from their other Jewish messianic Christian peers who did not share their views about the divinity of Christ. He comments:

> In summary, the clash with their Jewish opponents likely led Johannine Christians to emphasize Jesus' divine status

---

104 John 1:14, 18; 17:1-5.

105 April D. DeConick, *Voices of the Mystics: Early Christian Discourse in the Gospels of John and Thomas and Other Ancient Christian Literature*, Sheffield: Sheffield Academic Press (2001), pp. 68-85.

106 Larry W. Hurtado, *Lord Jesus Christ: Devotion to Jesus in Earliest Christianity*, Grand Rapids: Eerdmans (2005), pp. 400-402.

and attributes, his heavenly origins, and his exclusive significance over against all other figures and religious claims in Jewish tradition. The clash may also have been one factor that disposed Johannine Christians to cultivate religious experiences in which the Spirit-Advocate could reveal to them the glories of Jesus. Because of these revelatory experiences, they were likely emboldened in their faith and were prompted further to emphasize his divinity over against detractors. These responses to the external threat of Jewish opposition may also help us to understand some of the circumstances that contributed to the subsequent Christological controversy in Johannine Christianity reflected in 1 John.[107]

Hurtado's suggestions are insightful and broadly helpful in the way they enable us to understand what is likely to have caused the rift. It probably became clear that the Johannine group's theology embraced a higher Christology of the divine origins of the Christ than more conservative Jewish Christians were willing to entertain. It is quite possible that the group from which they split were also messianic Christians, who may have preferred an adoption theology for Jesus' origins. (Adoption theology holds the view that Jesus was not divine, but that as a result of His perfect life He was adopted by the Father to become His Son in a special sense which made Him universal lord of creation under God.)

A close reading of the first letter of John finds the writer warning the Johannine church to beware of those who once fellowshipped with them,[108] who had become what are called by John 'antichrists', meaning those who put themselves in the place of Christ, or against Christ. While the Johannine Christians did not overplay their divine Word theology, it fitted, broadly speaking, into the personification traditions of wisdom literature found in such passages as Proverbs 8:20-28. However, John's community almost certainly took this wisdom theology beyond the limits of the wisdom tradition, which

---

[107] Hurtado, *Lord Jesus Christ*, p. 407.
[108] 1 John 2:18-19.

had developed in the contemporary Judaism of his day. Jesus, as the wisdom of God, had not been Yahweh's first created work, but He was God Himself in the view of John's churches. This was contrary to beliefs held in the mainstream Judaism of the first century. No one, king or priest, would be the subject of apotheosis in Judaism such as was found in the Greco–Roman culture. (Apotheosis refers to the way a human king was transformed upon death to become one of the gods in a pantheon: for example, Augustus Caesar was deified upon his death in popular religious society of the time.)

The concept of the Word being the agent of creation in John 1:3 was developed with the view that Christ was divine.[109] To more conservative monotheistic messianic Jews of the period, this would have clearly smacked of ditheism (belief in two gods). It was this heightened Christology (making Jesus divine) that led the Johannine church to become a sectarian group that split off from other Jesus followers who did not think He was divine (I am using the term 'sectarian' in its sociological sense, to refer to a particular group that is segmented from another group). Hurtado's view of the Johannine church paints a bold picture of those who belonged to it. Encouraged by their charismatic experiences of the Spirit, and convinced that the Divine Word was indeed to be worshipped as God in unity with the Father, they held the bold conviction that they shared in the mission of God's Spirit to bring glory to the divine Christ whom they worshipped as the revelation of the Father's heart.[110]

Hurtado's view clearly allows for this church to have been bold in their missiology, although he recognises that they also found part of their identity in what they did not believe, by making comparison of their beliefs to those held by the other messianic Jewish Christians with whom they had once fellowshipped. Hurtado does not minimise the strong anti-Jewish flavour of the gospel, although he helpfully recognises that its use of the polemical word 'Jew' is meant to represent the Jewish authorities who were opposed to

---

[109] John 1:1, 3.
[110] Hurtado, *Lord Jesus Christ*, pp. 400-402.

Jesus, rather than all Jews in general. Rather sadly, the gospel has often been cited by people of the Jewish faith to be an anti-Jewish and racist document.[111] However, with great respect to their sensitivities, I would argue that, given that the Johannine church probably consisted of Aramaic speaking Jews and Hellenist Greek speaking Jews, the Jewish Christian group for whom the gospel was written could not have been against their own race. Rather they were reacting to Jewish authorities who were perceived to be against Christ, and to their own convictions about the divine person of Christ.

Graham Stanton takes a more cautious view of John's church. If Hurtado may be said to allow for a bold, outward-looking missional church, Stanton reverses the psychological reading to imply a more inward-looking church, on the defensive because they felt under attack by those who had expelled them from the synagogues. In his reading of the church behind the gospel, he suggests the members considered that people of their own race, as well as pagans, were against them:

> At least some members of the evangelist's communities have parted company painfully with local synagogues. Down through history minority religious groups which have parted with the 'parent' group have tended to become inward-looking and isolated from the world 'outside'.[112]

I would argue that there is a strong rejection theme in the gospel. The prologue begins by stating that the Word (Christ) was rejected by His own people.[113] The Nicodemus passage talks of the difference between Jesus' view of things compared to the view of

---

[111] Evidence of the so-called anti-Jewish propaganda that is pointed to by those who make this claim is to be found in passages like John 8:44.
[112] Graham Stanton, *The Gospels of Jesus*, Oxford: Oxford University Press (2002), p. 117.
[113] John 1:11.

Nicodemus as 'teacher of Israel' (i.e. teacher of other Jews).[114] This smacks of a definite dig at contemporary opponents to John's churches. Jesus engages in a number of heated debates with the 'Jews', who are clearly cast against Him because of His claims to equality with God.[115] They seek to stone Him for His blasphemous claims.[116] Jesus is crucified because the Jewish authorities demand it.[117] However, the gospel has pro-Jewish elements as well. When the woman met with Jesus at the well of Sychar, she asks about the proper place of worship.[118] The writer of the gospel adds the note to Jesus' response to the woman that the Jerusalem temple is the proper place for worship. Jesus then tells her that anyone can worship God through His Spirit in any place in the new order of things to come after His resurrection and ascension.[119] When Jesus raises Lazarus from the dead, observant Jews comment on 'how he loved him' because Jesus wept.[120] Jesus' first disciples are Jews as well, and they are not written off for their ethnic origins.

On balance, I would argue that although the Johannine church was facing challenges because of its belief that Jesus was divine, it had not lost its deep spiritual experience of the risen Lord, by the charismatic encounters of believers with the Spirit.[121] Moreover, 1 John demonstrates that the church was based on strong fellowship structures that existed between its people, which it valued and sought to maintain.[122] The Johannine churches were not a set of communities that had closed their fellowships to outsiders. The desire to protect the fellowships of these churches from corrupting influences came from a pastoral concern for their members, so that their core values and beliefs would not be undermined. In reality,

---

[114] John 3:10.
[115] John 5:18, RSV.
[116] John 8:59.
[117] John 18:38-40.
[118] John 4:1-26.
[119] John 4:19-24.
[120] John 11:35-37.
[121] Hurtado, *Lord Jesus Christ,* pp. 400-402.
[122] 1 John 1:3; 2:18-27; 4:7-21.

the Johannine churches were seeking to maintain their high views of Christ the divine Son, as well as His relationship with His heavenly Father. This fellowship of intimacy which Father and Son enjoyed was to include those who belonged to His family. Father and Son are defined in the gospel by the way They share intimacy (see John 5:19-20). The Spirit is part of this intimacy, as it is by the Spirit that the Father and Son make Their home in believers' hearts.[123] As I mentioned earlier, the Father gave Himself to the world through the Son. God wants His people to own their place in His family as much as we belong to God and God belongs to us.

The view is that the Father who loves the Son also loves His children which is evidenced by the fact that the Father sacrifices His most loved Son for the sake of His children. The impact of this theology of sacrifice is huge: the Father and Son value and love Their people as much as Father and Son love each other. Those who belong to God's family are to love in similar manner to the love of God for them.

I want to dig a bit deeper now, by asking two practical questions which have to some extent been addressed in what I have just written. But it is important to focus our attention more directly on them. Firstly, what picture of God did the Johannine church have? Secondly, how did this Christian community experience God in the light of its intimate spiritual connection with Father, Son and Spirit?

Knowledge of what God is like

In order to understand John's gospel in terms of its relational theology of fellowship, it is important to consider the often-used Greek word *ginosko*. *Ginosko*, in its classical usage, has to do with knowledge of something that comes through a methodological scientific approach, by which something can be known based on verifiable empirical investigation.[124] The relational interpretation of

---

[123] John 14:1-3, 15-25.

[124] Bultmann, R., γινωσκω, Gerhard Kittel (ed.), *Theological Dictionary of the New Testament*, Vol. 1, Grand Rapids: Eerdmans (1979), p. 694.

the New Testament usage of the verb has almost certainly been overplayed, where it is claimed that it represents knowledge that comes out of personal relationships wherever it is used in New Testament writings.

However, the word does take on this kind of relational meaning in John's writings more generally, compared to its use elsewhere.[125] It is true that the verb plays a greater role in John's gospel and first epistle, than 'in any other early Christian writings'.[126] It is used in a twofold sense in John. Firstly, it describes 'emphatically the relationship to God and to Jesus as a personal fellowship in which each is decisively determined by the other in his own existence'.[127] Secondly, the meaning is then extended beyond the Father–Son relationship, as Bultmann classically defined it in Kittel:

> As the relationship between the Father and the Son, which elsewhere can be described as ειναι εν [einai en – being in] (Jh. 10:38; 14:11; 17:21; cf. esp. 1 Jn. 2:3, 5; 5:20) and even 'εν ειναι [hen einai – in being] (Jh. 10:30), is a mutual γινωσκειν [ginoskein – to know], so is the relationship between Jesus and His own (Jh. 10:14 f., 27; cf. 7:29; 8:55), which can also be described as ειναι εν (Jn. 15.1 ff.; 17:21).[128]

What Bultmann goes on to demonstrate is the quality of the relational fellowship that exists between Father and Son in John's theological view of Their relationship. It is based on intimate Father–Son love in terms of God's love in action, coming from the Father to the Son, from the Son to the Father, and from the Father and the Son to the world. This love in action is the energy behind God's self-revelation in Christ, where Christ is the love-gift of God to the world. The power that motivates the Johannine community is defined as the power of God's selfless love, rather than in terms

---

[125] Kittel, *Theological Dictionary of the New Testament*, p. 711.
[126] Kittel, *Theological Dictionary of the New Testament*, p. 711.
[127] Kittel, *Theological Dictionary of the New Testament*, p. 711.
[128] Kittel, *Theological Dictionary of the New Testament*, p. 711.

of the use of abusive power motivating God or His community. The motivation of God is to gift the world with His active grace, aimed at bringing people to faith through the love-gift of eternal life in Christ. This love-gift is based on the love of God that is always actively at work for each of His creatures. Hence this relational knowledge has as its object the eternal abiding of each follower with the Father and Son, as part of Their family. We may add the further conviction that the Spirit is also part of the Trinity family so that we will always belong in Their family by the motivating love of the Spirit. The kind of knowledge which is based on this motivational love means that those who encounter the revealed Christ obtain 'awareness of being loved'.[129]

John 17:3 tells us that eternal life is defined by knowing God (see John 17:3 in the broader context of chapters 13–17). Jesus made this statement, which informs us that it is not quantity of life which attracted the Johannine church to the Father's family, but rather the quality of the love bonds which motivated God to send His Son and Spirit in order to base His family on sacrificial love and service. Quality of life is more important to our missional communities than the quantity of people we evangelise without the quality of God's selfless love defining our fellowship together. The 'awareness' of this love also motivates God's love towards the Son through the Spirit towards the Father, as well as towards each of the persons of the Trinity towards each other. Gift-love (*agape*) is the active will of the Father that sends the Son and the Spirit to make all of us see ourselves as part of God's eternal, all-encompassing family. The revelation of God's love was a practical spiritual reality that John's churches regularly experienced. People lived for each other, offering love as service to one another as defined by the Father, Son and Spirit. I would also say that the people of these churches expressed that same love in their relationships with faith-seekers (of course, the term 'Trinity' is never used in John's gospel).

This same love is to motivate the Spirit's sending of God's people to transform the world. Another way the gospel speaks of the

---

[129] Kittel, *Theological Dictionary of the New Testament*, p. 711.

quality of this relational knowledge of God's love that they experience together is to say that it causes followers to 'remain' in God's love (John 15:9; see also John 17:26; 1 John 4:16). The knowledge of the Father's love for the Son, and the Son's love for the Father, is expressed directly to the world to which Christ has been sent – as God's love incarnate. Christ is the God-man whom the whole world is to come to know by seeing that same love displayed through Christians towards them (John 3:16). Of course, John's gospel asserts that not all receive that love. Knowledge of God, based on God's sacrificial love demonstrated through the sacrifice of Christ, will motivate followers to return that love to God and others, according to 1 John 4:7-10.

It is also vital to be clear that God's love is the way that Christian communities can unanimously overcome the devil (or evil personified), whose very nature is defined by selfish pursuit of egotistically motivated behaviours without thought of putting God or others first.[130] To really experience the joy of being liberated to live for God and others means we never have to think about getting things our way, because our needs will be met by others giving sacrificially to us. This motivating *agape* love also makes it possible for God's love to be received from God and others, when it is focused in the direction of all those in the world that God loves, both believers and non-believers. We need to learn to receive sacrificial gifts from others graciously, and not as charity, as much as we want to serve others with gifts.

This is a hard lesson for us to learn in Western society because we have to earn our living through hard work. It is also true in non-Western society. The difference is that in the West the supremacy of the cult of the individual has bred a certain type of prideful independence: most of us want to plough our own furrow and fiercely resist any whiff of the notion that others might see us as lacking in self-sufficiency, or being in any way needy! God's love turns this narrative of hard work upside down, and rather changes our picture of love into giving and receiving gratefully from God

---

[130] 1 John 4:4-6.

and others, as we take part in this giving and receiving as a primary kingdom narrative that needs to define our MT-shaped families.

Love that is received becomes an awareness of 'being loved'. This was true for a gay young man who came to one of the churches I know. He loved God and wanted to be given recognition for his Christian faith. He had been condemned by some Christian groups for being gay. He found a welcome in the group I have in mind. He was welcomed and took part in the church without feeling condemned for his sexual orientation. (There is a difference between being gay by orientation and being a practicing homosexual, in the view of many evangelical churches.)

This is important for us to consider. The picture of the missionary God portrayed by a growing number of churches today has caused a number of them to recognise that God welcomes all people, whatever their challenges, to belong to His family. God the missionary does not call perfect people to belong to His family. Without doubt, there will be many Christians who struggle with their sexuality and how they engage in sexual behaviour. Sexual lust is something Christians are not immune to. The large missional question for me is, 'How can we help each other to become like Jesus, who is the picture of God that we need to model our lives on?' I want to help people to get to know what He is like rather than spending my time telling people what is wrong with them. As one senior and elderly pastor once said to me, 'Andrew, when you point your finger at someone else, there are three pointing back at you.'

This discussion has demonstrated the grounds of John's *missio Dei/missio Trinitatis* thinking. It is based on the Father, Son and Holy Spirit's love that motivates God's people to extend it beyond themselves, to express the message to others that God wants everyone who will trust Him to become part of His family. Christian missional communities take on their mission in the shape of the Father who sends the Son as a love message to the world. The mission of the Father acts as a propelling love that offers unconditional, non-judgemental love to others. God is love, and there is no room for hating others; to do so is not to have the love of

God motivating our inner lives and souls.[131] Rather, we use blame directed towards others so that we can feel better about our own weaknesses, which we do not want to be healed in ourselves, so that we can hold on to our sense of control.

We judge ourselves, in other words, and continue to wallow in our own self-inflicted misery because of our intrinsic selfishness when we bar access of the Spirit's inner love for us to our souls. The Spirit is love in action. The people of God who share intimacy with other people start to behave in new ways when they provide gifts of service to others and receive them from others as well. It causes us to transcend our own selfishness and individualism. This can lead to a more sustainable, love-based family which will last beyond our finite lives into eternity. According to Paul in 1 Corinthians 13:1–14:1, love is the meaning of life and the kingdom of God. If we do not have God's gift-love then we will not want to be part of His eternal kingdom. The *imago Trinitatis* in the human genome is based on the imprint of the nature of the Trinity within humanity. If we do not share in Their eternal sacrificial love, then we cannot be part of Their eternal family. This is the choice we all have to make: to love others and to receive love from others and from God.

What is God like? I suggest that God is like Trinity – the Father sends His love-gift in Jesus. Jesus sends the Spirit as the love-gift, who charismatically communicates God's heart of sacrificial love to all people without showing partiality. There is no greater satisfaction in God's family than when we share with the Father His deep satisfaction in seeing others transcend their selfish limitations, becoming more than they were before. This is what we are designed to do. The design is operationalised when we live for God and others, taking joy in their development and growth. We may lose sight of ourselves at times, but our spiritual connection with the inner Spirit of God helps us to remain critically self-aware so that we do not lose ourselves, because each person only exists as a real person when they are defined by knowing other persons different to themselves, making them further aware of themselves as a

---

[131] 1 John 4:19-21.

person loved by God and His people. In other words, we need each other. Not even God exists as a single deity, but the persons of the Trinity joined by the one eternal being of God are real persons in relationship to each other and to us. God can only meaningfully exist for Godself and ourselves if He is a personal being, who lives in relationship based on the communion of persons. (See chapter 7 for more discussion of this topic.)

> **Identity based on helping others to become like Jesus modelled in the community!**
>
> Riverside Family Church – Southampton
>
> 'At Riverside Family Church we have four key values which shape our vision.
>
> **Worship:** We believe that we are designed to live our lives to love God and our neighbours. We express this love by knowing Jesus as our Lord and Saviour and by *living the kind of life He lived*.
>
> **Relationship:** The Bible describes the church as a body where people share their lives through mutual support, encouragement, caring for one another and sharing our faith. *We are a family.*
>
> **Membership:** We all need to belong because this is really important to us. But being part of a church is not like being a member of a club. Being part of Riverside Family Church is about *being committed to a family* where we can grow and support each other.
>
> **Discipleship:** Being a Christian is about learning and sharing our lives with others and helping them to discover Jesus too. Christianity is a shared life where we use our gifts to *share the good news of Jesus*.'
>
> http://www.riversidefamilychurch.org.uk/corevalues.htm

I suggest that it is the Father's sacrificial interpersonal nature of love that wants everyone to whom it reaches out, to eternally participate in God's family. The Father has many children, according to John; children who will be united by their love for

Christ to the Father by the inner agency of the Spirit. The Spirit motivates their hearts to live interpersonally with others whom they serve and from whom they receive loving service. This is the basis of the kingdom of God society, which I believe is at the foundation of the MT's most sacred purposes. These people participate together in sharing God's love with each other, where each one in the community is aware of being loved and valued as they value and love each other and their God. The picture of God in John's gospel is based on the picture of a God who gives eternal life to all those who want to trust in the love of Father, Son and Spirit. As 1 John so clearly puts it:

> Beloved, let us love one another; for love is of God, and he who loves is born of God and knows God. He who does not love does not know God [experientially, in other words: remember how *ginosko* is used in the Johannine documents]; for God is love. In this the love of God was made manifest among us, that God sent his only Son into the world, so that we might live through him. In this is love, not that we loved God but that he loved us and sent his Son to be the expiation for our sins. Beloved, if God so loved us, we also ought to love one another. No man has ever seen God; if we love one another, God abides in us and his love is perfected in us.[132]

1 John offers a particularly fine hermeneutical (interpretational) cypher, by which we can interpret some of the gospel's theological language into the practicalities of what needs to inform our daily lives as missional disciple-makers. The saying 'like father like son' means that we, as disciple-makers, will portray God's love to others through words and deeds that will provide them with a practical picture of the God upon whom we model our lives. We are not to be utilitarian, just behaving in loving ways in order to clinically do our duty without passion for Jesus and those for whom He died; we actually need to authentically and genuinely care for others, in a

---

[132] 1 John 4:7-12, RSV.

similar way to how God cares for them with His infinite self-giving love (called *agape* in the New Testament documents).

I know an Indian Christian family who have had significant impact on white working-class youth. The way they have achieved this is by living their lives alongside these young people, playing sports with them and eating food with them, and these young people are becoming Christians. Whenever I meet with members of this family I am deeply impressed with the love of God that shines through them. 'God is love' is practically portrayed for us in the gospel of John, to mean that we serve others through selfless, loving acts, not expecting something in return, but joyfully receiving love-motivated gifts, as this means we can intentionally have lasting, interactive, reciprocal friendships.

Deep intimacy with Father, Son and Holy Spirit motivates our lives. In the sections that follow we will look at the first epistle of John in order to expand John's picture of the God who loves us, through the actions of His self-revelation in Christ among people with whom He interacted during His earthly ministry.

The Spirit as intimate voice of the Son

Hurtado suggests that John's gospel and first epistle contain clues as to the spiritual practices used by John's churches.[133] Given the claims of both documents that the Spirit was still revealing the things of Christ to His people, it will be useful to see what artefacts of these practices can be excavated from these texts. Hurtado recognises that:

> John 14-16 is the most sustained treatment of the relationship of the Spirit and Jesus in any Christian writing of the first century, and this material has distinctive features.[134]

---

133 Hurtado, *Lord Jesus Christ,* p. 400.
134 Hurtado, *Lord Jesus Christ,* p. 398.

It is important to note Hurtado's key points about the role of the Spirit in these chapters. Firstly, people in these churches have encounters with the Spirit who communicates specific things to them, which the first generation of disciples could not bear. Hurtado suggests that the gospel contains revelatory communications from the ascended Jesus which John potentially includes in his gospel. Moreover, I would suggest that the Spirit of Christ continues to reveal new authoritative truths to God's people throughout the ongoing historical revelation of God to the church in church traditions and Christian experience. Secondly, the Spirit may be said to communicate to the community in a semantically coherent way – i.e., new things are revealed which were not known to the church before. Thirdly, the Spirit 'is heavily focused on, producing in Jesus' followers deeper insights into Jesus'[135] and His significance, and a fuller appreciation of His teachings. I would call this an interpretative role, whereby the meaning of the Jesus event is explained in new or more deeply reflective ways by those who have prophetically received revelations from the Spirit. Fourthly, the mission of the Spirit towards the world (16:7-11) and among Jesus' followers (16:12-15) aims to 'prove the world wrong' with respect to sin and judgement to come (16:8), because of the world's failure to perceive the significance and effects of Christ's appearance and the Father's work in his ministry (vs 10-11). Hurtado concludes:

> We may say, therefore, that as Jesus serves as spokesman and agent of the Father, so these references to the Spirit in John 14-16 portray the Spirit as advocate, spokesman, and agent of Jesus.[136]

When my wife Jenny and I first moved to Lowestoft in the 1990s we led an aging church which had no young families, children or young people. We prayed about this a lot – what had God sent us

---

[135] Hurtado, *Lord Jesus Christ,* p. 400.
[136] Hurtado, *Lord Jesus Christ,* p. 399.

to Lowestoft to do for Him? We continued to ask this question for about six months. Then one day, as I walked on one of the beaches in Lowestoft, I heard a powerful inner voice say to me, 'I will reach families through their children. Do a holiday summer club.' We both became convinced that this was God's voice telling us to run a holiday club for children. The church had done nothing like this for years. Without recounting the whole story, the church subsequently found itself with about 40 children coming to church each week, and parents were also coming to take part in some seeker-friendly services. I could write much more, but what this illustrates is that the Spirit guides us to know the heart of God for the people among whom we live. God uses words of prophecy to guide us on His mission. Families were at the heart of His communication to us. Indeed, this is part of the story that helped us to see how important it is for our churches to portray a picture of the Trinity family, which in turn needs to inform our behaviours to portray the love of God to people with whom we form friendships. This prophetically motivated love has to be the fabric of our Christian lives and experiences.

How should we respond to this practical theology of the Spirit? We need to take it seriously. We need to develop sensitivities to the work of the Spirit in our lives and in the lives of others. This will be uncomfortable, as the Spirit's role is not only to glorify Jesus; He also convicts people of 'sin and righteousness and judgement'.[137] He will work in the interior lives of persons who come under conviction. There will necessarily be radical evidence of people changing their beliefs and behaviours when these have fallen short of God's selfless love. This needs to motivate our communities to be the hermeneutic of the sacrificial love that motivates the eternal nature of the Trinity's family that needs to inform our Christian communities. We now live the life of the future age in the consciousness of our present community. We have already been transported spiritually into the future age of God's eternal family so that we live the future life of God's *agape* love in the present world.

---

[137] John 16:8.

The church needs to be robust enough to have people join them who are carrying challenging baggage; believers will need to walk alongside them and help them overcome difficult life situations. Among the contemporary challenges of life in the West are drug addiction, sex addiction, alcoholism, relationship breakdown and abuse. John's churches must have framed their supportive networks around gift-love put into practical helpful actions. It was unacceptable not to offer practical love to those in need – to do so was to essentially 'hate' a brother because sacrificial love had not motivated supportive behaviours:

> If any one says, 'I love God,' and hates his brother, he is a liar; for he who does not love his brother whom he has seen, cannot love God whom he has not seen. And this commandment we have from him, that he who loves God should love his brother also.[138]

The character of Father, Son and Spirit

The picture of God portrayed in the gospel is astounding. The most revealing passage regarding the character of the Son of God is found in John 13. John 13 records its own version of the Last Supper event that Jesus hosted for His disciples on the night before His death on Calvary. He was conscious of it. People often say the most important things to those they love from their deathbeds. This is the time to communicate the most intimate things that shape the love we hold for each other.

The narrative of John 13 is simple enough to summarise. The disciples are all seated at the table of fellowship, but there is no servant present to wash their feet. None of the disciples wishes to wash the others' feet. Hence Jesus de-robes himself to His undergarments and proceeds to wash each of the disciples' feet. This act is unthinkable to Peter, who tries to resist. How could he allow his Lord to act as his servant?

---

[138] 1 John 4:20-21, RSV.

This event had a profound effect on the early Johannine church's understanding of the character of Christ and the way in which character needed to motivate their own fellowships. Jesus tells Peter that if He is not permitted to wash his feet, then he will have no part with Jesus. As a result, Peter permits his Lord to wash his feet. After all the disciples' feet have been washed, Jesus takes His place back at the table. In His next words to the disciples we obtain a keen insight into John's vision of the character of the Lord Jesus Christ, which framed the picture of God that his churches held dear.

> When he had washed their feet, and taken his garments, and resumed his place, he said to them, 'Do you know what I have done to you? You call me Teacher and Lord; and you are right, for so I am. If I then, your Lord and Teacher, have washed your feet, you also ought to wash one another's feet. For I have given you an example, that you also should do as I have done to you. Truly, truly, I say to you, a servant is not greater than his master; nor is he who is sent greater than he who sent him. If you know these things, blessed are you if you do them.'[139]

It is not many verses later that Jesus declares to Philip that if he has seen Jesus he has also seen what the Father is like (John 14:8, 9). The gospel needs to be interpreted in the light of its overall revelatory theme. The Son only does what He sees the Father doing.[140] Jesus was sent by the Father to make known God's selfless sacrificial love for His children. What is the character of the Son of this Father who sent Him? As the disciples' 'Teacher and Lord', He gives them an example to follow. This example comes from the very nature of the heart of God, displayed in the life of Christ. Christ has come to serve and not to be served. He has come to reveal what the Father is like. God lives to serve, rather than exercising His power to manipulate and force His people to do what He commands.

---

[139] John 13:12-17, RSV.
[140] John 5:19.

God's love is defined by service. This is what the Father, Son and Spirit are like. God as Trinity lives to serve God's other persons and all the persons God has created. God does not need us, but He does want to serve us. True love is defined as love which loves others first, before others love Christ the initiator of God's love in action.[141] God in Christ is the humble Lord who is servant of all that He has made and sustains through acts of service. When we come to know this God, our service to Him and to each other will flow in an eternal circuit of beneficence which will define God's sustainable eternal family, of which we are a part. The kingdom of the Trinity can only be entered by those who live to serve as God's self-extending gift-love flows between the three persons of the Trinity and the persons They have as sons and daughters in God's family.

God comes to the lost world and seeks out His lost children. The fatherly love of God exists to bless and serve others. The very nature of Father, Son and Holy Spirit is defined as each of the persons of God living to serve the other persons of the Trinity, as well as God expressing that same love in serving creation by continually upholding its existence and freeing its children to consciously transcend themselves in relationship with others and with the relational God.

God's very nature is sacrificial love that serves others through practical deeds of love in action. This kind of *agape* love also needs to define the way the people of God treat each other and others they come to know. We live to serve, because the Master of the cosmos lives to serve. This sets out a very different version of power theology, compared to what the world considers power to be.

The power exercised by God does not seek to get its own way; rather, by the very act of giving love as service, people can come to trust that the most powerful being in the universe is not a dominating tyrant who wants to force them to do things for Him. I fear that much of what Evangelicals and Protestants paint is a dire picture of a God who needs us to suck up to Him. God the Trinity is not threatened by us. God wants, rather than needs, to help us

---

[141] 1 John 4:10.

119

find the deep meaning of life that His perfect being and infinite knowledge of reality portrays to be love based on *perichoresis* (a harmonious dance based on an interdependent set of transparent relationships that form the life-cycle of the persons of the Trinity). This is indeed a profound vision, from which the missional church needs to take its identity.

If we serve others by sacrificial acts of service motivated by God's selfless love, we will serve others rather than using others to get what we want for ourselves. What a different kind of missiology it would have been during the colonial period of world missions if the church had not entangled itself in the imperial power narratives of the European empires that raped the natural resources of the peoples they invaded. We need to repent of our own self-centred pictures of God, where we treat God as a vending machine who provides for our needs. Rather, we need to express a new picture of God through our behaviours, where we seek to sacrificially love others despite the personal cost to ourselves, just as God in Christ portrayed, for the whole cosmos to witness, His sacrificial and selfless heart of love. I seek to model some of this love in my work with students who take the courses offered by ForMission College.[142] We try to take time to ensure that they all receive the best possible educational experiences that display the heart of God through the courses we offer.

The Johannine church known by its qualitative love

The Johannine church had its own particular kind of vulnerability. It had gone through a very challenging period in which its members had been expelled from the Jewish community in Galilee after the council of Jamnia, because of their seeming ditheistic beliefs. The Johannine church was having to go through a healing process, as we all need to, as its people felt deeply rejected and betrayed by

---

[142] ForMission College. Available at http://formission.org.uk/ (accessed 28th September 2015).

their Jewish compatriots. God helps our communities to go on a journey over time, moving from an inner, self-directed focus based on fear of pain and hurt towards an ever-increasing meta-vista of inclusivity of all others whom God loves impartially.

We are all, already, part of this impartial loving kingdom community which I describe as the purpose of the MT. I was sent to help one church where there had been a rift between members. It took a long time for them to change their story from, 'We were betrayed' to being able to say, 'We want to welcome new people into our fellowship.' However, they did move to this new narrative once they had had time to grieve and recover from their feelings of betrayal. They needed to obtain new confidence that God loved them and that they loved each other. As their confidence grew, they started to embrace others into their faith community.

The hurt of John's churches is expressed in the language of hot debates between the Jews and Jesus in the narrative sections of his gospel. Jesus is often found to be in conflict with his Jewish brothers. He goes as far as declaring to them that they belong to a father other than Yahweh: 'You are of your father the devil.'[143] In John's records of Jesus' conflicts with the Jewish authorities, we find a kind of catharsis for the Johannine churches taking place. Like Jesus the Lord, they too have been deeply hurt and impacted by the rejection of the Jewish community to which they once belonged. How can they overcome this hurt and resist becoming bitter?

John provides the language of healing love which these churches need to hear as they go on their own journey, seeking to overcome their fear of being hurt again. Just as the Father, Son and Spirit are deeply joined in Their love for each other, and just as They express that love to those They have created, so must John's Christian community go beyond their hurts and bitterness and embrace the love of God that will free them to serve God, each other and new faith-seekers once more. This requires them to go through a process of forgiving those they feel have betrayed them before they can be fully ready to embrace others into their community. I believe they

---

[143] John 8:44-45.

were still welcoming faith-seekers to their churches, but it took time for the Johannine gospel's experiential narrative of God's love-based family to penetrate their fellowship and to transform it. The good news is that God works through our communities as they go on journeys of transition, flawed as they are, welcoming new people and discovering through this process of evangelisation just how much passion new people have for the God who has embraced them through His community. This same love that will bind John's churches together in deeper fellowship over time will also be the hallmark of God's divine presence, which welds them together as one, just as the Father and Son are said to be one in Their interpersonal relationship.[144]

John's churches can still reach out to embrace others who are not part of their community. Just as the Father sent the Son, so now Jesus sends them by God's Spirit – sending them to reveal the heart of the Father to a lost world. Jesus declared after the supper:

> A new commandment I give to you, that you love one another; even as I have loved you, that you also love one another. By this all men will know that you are my disciples, if you have love for one another.[145]

Notice the emphasis on knowing, which the display of united love between the disciples will portray to others. It is the *ginosko* kind of knowing we are talking about here. People who as yet do not know the Lord Jesus will come to know His love exhibited towards them by His followers. As Lesslie Newbigin classically stated, the 'local church is the hermeneutic of the gospel'.[146] Our missional communities express God's love as service given to faith-seekers, so that they can be guided by the Spirit to see themselves as belonging to Trinity's family. The catharsis that was needed to uproot any bitterness from the Johannine church, because of its

---

[144] John 17:1-21.
[145] John 13:34-35, RSV.
[146] Lesslie Newbigin, *The Gospel in a Pluralist society*, Grand Rapids: Eerdmans (1989), chapter 18.

expulsion from among its compatriot Jews was for its people to love each other, and to make that love known in acts of service to the faith-seeking peoples around it. They also needed to forgive their brothers and sisters who had expelled them from their community. The so-called Johannine Pentecost passage in the gospel beautifully sets the scene for what the missional church has been sent to do, as it takes the gospel's good news about God's family to the world:

> Jesus said to them again, 'Peace be with you. As the Father has sent me, even so I send you.' And when he had said this, he breathed on them, and said to them, 'Receive the Holy Spirit. If you forgive the sins of any, they are forgiven; if you retain the sins of any, they are retained.'[147]

Charismatic spiritual discernment and *missio Dei*

The previous paragraph sets the scene for suggestions of how John's churches probably received charismatic guidance from the Spirit in order to engage in the *missio Trinitatis*. Hurtado believes that the Johannine churches probably shared in the common heritage of the Christian charismatic tradition of the early church period. He proposes that the church received 'insights . . . experienced and received as prophetic revelations, the sorts of "charismatic" experiences of revealed "knowledge" and "wisdom",' as highlighted in Paul's writings.[148] The testimony in favour of the charismatic experience of this group of churches is also indicated in John 14:12-14, where Jesus tells His disciples that they will perform miracles greater in scope than Christ Himself did while He was on the earth. Hurtado comments that 'the scope of expectation for miraculous powers was considerable!'[149] Moreover, the New Testament scholar David Aune has demonstrated that Christian worship was the normal place for prophetic apocalyptic charismatic

---

[147] John 20:21-23, RSV.

[148] Hurtado, *Lord Jesus Christ*, p. 400; 1 Corinthians 12:4-11.

[149] Hurtado, *Lord Jesus Christ*, p. 400.

revelations of the Spirit to take place.[150] This seems well attested to in the gospel and the first epistle.[151] We have already considered Jesus' promise that the Paraclete would reveal things to the future church. Moreover, 1 John says:

> I write this to you about those who would deceive you; but the anointing which you received from him abides in you, and you have no need that any one should teach you; as his anointing teaches you about everything, and is true, and is no lie, just as it has taught you, abide in him.[152]

We notice the pastoral concern and emphasis of the epistle. There are some who wish to 'deceive' these churches. The anointing of the Holy Spirit in each of their hearts guards them from false teaching. There is obviously still some conflict between this church and the group they have left. The epistle describes the central point of contention as the claim that the divine Son of God had become incarnate as a revelation of the Father.[153] John informs his readers that they have the charismatic anointing of the Spirit, sent by Christ, who will teach them aright and keep them established in their relationship with God. We are probably meant to understand this anointing to be provided by the indwelling presence of the Holy Spirit in each of the believers' internal psyches. Moreover, it is not hard to take the next step, to include the gift of prophecy as an essential component of the way the church obtained specific messages of how it was to proceed as it partook in the *missio Dei*. John's churches pictured God as a missionary deity.

---

[150] David E. Aune, *The Cultic Setting of Realized Eschatology in Early Christianity*, Leiden: Brill (1972), p. 28.
[151] John 16:12-16; 1 John 2:26-27.
[152] 1 John 2:26-27, RSV.
[153] 1 John 4:1-6.

Conclusions

Those who share their lives deeply with God through the indwelling Spirit of Christ will themselves become a picture of what God is like in some important ways as they treat others in gracious ways. God is pictured, to some extent, as a family in John's gospel. Father, Son and Spirit form the divine family on which all earthly families are to model their lives. Christians belong to the MT's family. I suggest that the *missio Trinitatis* needs to frame the identities of all of God's sons and daughters as those who belong to God, and to whom God belongs.

We are the Father's children. This is the picture of God our communities need to portray as the practical applied theology of the MT. God is a caring, supportive and wise Father whom we can trust. This will only happen if we form our family identities by all seeking to participate in fellowship and trust-based intimacy – shared together.

In the next chapter we will consider how the portrayal of God the missionary Trinity came about.

Part 3

Theological and historical foundations to the development of a picture of God expressed as *missio Trinitatis* and the Multicultural Trinity

Chapter 6
How *missio Dei* became the mission of the Trinity

All good practical historical theologies begin at the beginning. *Missio Dei* as a theological idea had a beginning. If you find yourself having to raise funds for a project, or to fund your ministry, you will need a marketing strategy that will make the case for why people should give to your ministry or project. Part of such a strategy will include a clear, compelling description of what you want the funds for; it will need to prove convincingly that it is worthy.

Missio Dei as a slogan

Theologians talk of apologetics,[154] which partly has to do with 'selling' or defending the Christian faith to those who are hostile to it. The aim is to provide good reasons why people should invest in a relationship with God (if you will forgive the analogy). The idea that God is a missionary was first used as a marketing idea (so to speak), to help the German world missionary endeavours to raise support for missionary work outside of Germany. This began in the 1930s as a response to the great depression which impacted the world, beginning with the great crash in Wall Street. It did not, as such, come into usage based on a profound insight into God's nature. Rather, it was a slogan which painted a word picture of God as a missionary, the patron of the German missionary agencies who used the idea as a rallying cry to raise funds from potential Christian supporters.

---

[154] A reasoned defence of something, such as the Christian faith.

Reflection

- What slogans, word pictures or logos have you used to raise funds?

- What picture of God did you use, if at all, to create the rationale for your project?

- How effective was your fund-raising?

- How did your slogan become a key part of your ministry's identity as a result of using it often as the rallying cry to obtain supporters?

- How do supporters still rally around this marketing-based identity?

Record your reflections here

Often, the slogans we use to justify our projects actually become part of our identities as Christian communities. *Missio Dei* has become much more than a slogan to raise support for missionary work in today's environment. However, I fear it is used too often by some leaders as a slogan to support their own versions of missional ministry, which has much more to do with empowering their egos than with providing a helpful picture to shape their communities.

Let's take some time to consider how *missio Dei* was first understood, and how it has come to be used. The idea that God has a mission, which is His possession and in which we need to participate, is vital for us to explore, as I believe it is at the heart of God's very nature. It is important also to understand why *missio Dei* is such an important part of a missional community's picture of God, which will in turn shape that community's identity, beliefs and behaviours.

Charting the course of our journey

The idea that God Himself is a missionary is a central concept that is now frequently being used in many missional churches. The church does not own God's mission, to do as it wills with it. God owns it and calls us to participate. I have already pointed out that I prefer to speak metaphorically of the MT, which we may also link to *missio Trinitatis*. This is a word picture of the God who wants all peoples and nations in our Western society to be united because God's nature incorporates all those He has made to share in the likeness of *imago Trinitatis* as co-sharers in His cosmic family. I prefer MT as a practical missional theological idea to describe a new story that can be told about God, where He is portrayed as calling each cultural group to partner with Godself in intentional multicultural mission. The multicultural Christian community is a multi-voiced family.[155] I have spoken of it as a diverse kingdom forest where different trees and creatures draw from its rich environment to sustain their lives. The whole world as God's forest means that all peoples are called to make a choice to belong to the kingdom forest, in the terms we discussed in chapter 2.

In order to understand how we have moved from *missio Dei* theology as a narrative picture of God to *missio Trinitatis* and to my

---

155 Stuart and Sian Murray Williams, *Multi-Voiced Church,* Milton Keynes: Paternoster Press (2011), pp. 1-23.

metaphor of MT, we need to understand the history of how this new story of God's activity in mission was birthed as an idea, or slogan, in Germany in 1952.[156] It seems clear enough to some readers of the Bible that God is portrayed as having a plan (or mission), by which Godself has worked out His purposes in salvation history. The term *missio Dei* was first used in the 1930s (by Hartenstein), and then at Willingen widely in 1952. It picked up on what had been staring all previous generations in the face.

In this chapter and the one that follows we will explore how *missio Dei* has been used, as well as what I now think of as a new picture language that we need to use to describe God as MT as the church seeks to discern *missio Trinitatis*, which is meaningful to the Western multicultural, pluralistic environment.

Historical antecedents to a *Missio Dei* practical theology of mission

Missio Dei is increasingly being used by church leaders to describe their participation in God's mission, in and through their missional churches. The story of how the term came into being is sadly often glossed over.[157] The phrase is not to be found in the Bible, but the verbal root of *missio* is 'to send'. The verb 'to send' is used in Scripture, but in good English translations of the Bible the word 'mission' is never used to translate the Greek word meaning 'to send'.

John's gospel was particularly important as a canonical source that added weight to the development of the concept of the Trinity during the fourth, fifth and sixth centuries AD. And it was common

---

[156] John G. Flett, *The Witness of God: The Trinity, Missio Dei, Karl Barth, and the Nature of Christian Community*, Grand Rapids: Eerdmans (2010), pp. 123-162.
[157] For a thorough treatment of how *missio Dei* came into current mission thinking see Flett, *The Witness of God*.

for the church fathers of that period to recognise that Christ had been sent by the Father to put into operation His plan for the redemption of humankind. The church fathers relied on this gospel particularly, as they developed the idea of the Trinity at the councils of Nicaea, Constantinople, and so on. Trinitarian thought may be said to be implicit in John's assertion that the Father sent the Son, and the Son and the Father sent the Spirit.[158]

We begin our historical journey of *missio Dei* with some broad brush strokes of how we might think of

mission, where God is pictured as a sending deity. The Greek word used in John's gospel for 'to send' is *apostello*. The idea that Godself sends His Son and the Spirit to complete His plan to save humankind is part of a description of the roles that the persons in the Trinity could be said to fulfil (called the 'economic Trinity'). The Father is the source of mission, as He sends the Son to save the

---

[158] Peter R. Holmes, *Trinity in Human Community: Exploring Congregational Life in the Image of the Social Trinity*, Milton Keynes: Paternoster (2006), p. 52.

world and to bring believers into His eternal family.[159] When the Son completed His mission to save humanity during His life, death and resurrection, He then returned to His heavenly Father who had sent Him. Father and Son send the Spirit to continue the work of Christ in the world, until the climax of history when Christ will return to finally redeem His people.[160] At this time Christ will fully establish the eternal kingdom of God.[161] In this sense, *apostello* describes the work of Christ and the Spirit, as sent by the Father, as part of the divine plan of salvation. The Son is the redeemer and the Spirit connects God to His people and the people of God to Godself.

The English word 'apostle' is actually taken from the Greek noun used to describe Christ's apostles – *apostolos* – which takes on the meaning of 'messenger'. The original koine Greek speaks of someone who has been 'sent with a message as an ambassador to a foreign land'. It is interesting to note that the 12 apostles were sent by Jesus during His ministry not only to communicate the gospel, but also to heal the sick[162] and to proclaim release to the captives of Satan. Even Jesus is spoken of as an 'apostle' by the writer to the Hebrews.[163] This is not surprising, as the letter's theology positively articulates a sending purpose for the life and work of Christ, which is ongoing in His ascended life in God's presence. (A heavenly temple theology is implicit to the early Christian theological language of the Christians to whom the writer of Hebrews sent his tractate.[164]) It is also to be found in John's gospel, being used in this same sense with reference to Christ. For example:

> 'This is eternal life, that they may know you, the only true God, and Jesus Christ whom you have sent.'[165]

---

[159] John 17:1-5.
[160] John 16:5-16.
[161] Revelation 21:1-8.
[162] Luke 10:1-4.
[163] Hebrews 3:1.
[164] Hebrews 3:1-6.
[165] John 17:3.

Jesus does not refer to Himself as an apostle in this passage; in John's theology He is much more than just another apostle. However, Hebrews clearly demonstrates that Jesus was thought of by Jewish Christians as the ultimate apostle, probably based on a commonly accepted theology in the early church that He had been sent to fulfil God's mission. This must have derived from Jesus' claim to have been 'sent' by God.

At the most fundamental level, some theologians talk of God as a sending deity.[166] It is part of God's nature 'to send' His Son and 'to send' the Spirit. The term *missio Dei* arose out of recognition that God had sent His Son into the world, and by doing so He revealed Himself to humanity as a dynamically personal active being made up of persons. The famous theologian Karl Barth produced a theology of revelation that was built on the recognition that the coming of the Son from the Father into the world constituted an act of self-revelation.[167] Barth never used the term *missio Dei*, but he did speak of the action of God in the Latin phrase *actio Dei* ('God's action'). *Missio Dei* was later used, for the first time, by Barth's student Karl Hartenstein. Theologian John Flett notes that Hartenstein first used the phrase in an essay in 1934. He quotes from the essay:

> Mission today is called to examine itself in every way and always anew before God, to determine whether it is what it ought to be: missio Dei, the sending of God, that is the sending which Christ the Lord commands to the Apostles: 'As the Father has sent me, so I send you' – and the response to the call passed along by the apostles to the

---

[166] For example, Christopher J. H. Wright, *The Mission of God's People: A Biblical Theology of the Church's Mission*, Grand Rapids: Zondervan (2010), pp. 45-46, 66; Kirsteen Kim, *Joining in with the Spirit: Connecting World Church and Local Mission*, London: Epworth (2009), pp. 27-29; Timothy C. Tennent, *Invitation to World Missions: A Trinitarian Missiology for the Twenty-first Century*, Grand Rapids: Kregel Publications (2010), pp. 125-158.

[167] Barth Karl, *Church Dogmatics*, G. W. Bromiley and T. F.Torrance (eds.), *The Doctrine of the Word of God*, Vol. 1.1, Peabody: Hendricksen Publishers (2010 edition), pp. 295-332.

church of all times on the basis of its Word: 'Go into all the world.'[168]

Hartenstein wrote this in the light of the missionary funding crises that faced Protestant world missions in Germany during the 1930s. The church needed to recognise that the missionary task was based on a command to take the gospel to the nations. The call was for the church to respond by sending out missionaries. It seems obvious enough to Catholics, Protestants and Evangelicals etc. that Christ sent His disciples after His resurrection to:

> 'Go ... and make disciples of all nations, baptizing them in the name of the Father and of the Son and of the Holy Spirit, and teaching them to obey everything that I have commanded you. And remember, I am with you always, to the end of the age.'[169]

Reflection

How does the idea that God is a missionary affect the way you picture what God is calling your church to do?

Your thoughts and comments

---

[168] Flett, *The Witness of God*, p. 131.
[169] Matthew 28:19-20.

Historical case study of the development of *missio Dei* theology

John Flett offers three ways in which the term *missio Dei* has been used. It is important for us to understand how *missio Dei* theology first entered into the theology of mission, and what the three main views are. This will help us to grasp where the communitarian Trinitarian view of God's mission comes from. Flett helps us to understand these views clearly, as each offers a different answer to the question, 'Who is the agent of mission?'[170]

First of all, some theologians emphasise that God's mission does not need human agency in order for God to engage in mission in the world. God is sovereign and He does not need our help at all:

> Jesus' once-for-all completion of reconciliation has achieved everything the missionary act proposes. Missions achieve nothing, neither establishing the ground for, nor substantively contributing to, God's act.[171]

The implications are clear enough. Christ is thought to have achieved everything that is needed for all people to be saved, in a one-off redemptive act in history. The period between the resurrection and the second coming does not require the church to participate in God's mission. Missionary efforts have no impact on God completing His mission.

Secondly, other theologians argue that *missio Dei* requires God and His people to participate together in order to achieve His mission. God and His people have a shared history, where the Spirit of God is at work through the church, guiding its people and empowering them to participate in God's mission. This second option allows for the work of the Trinity. This is, for me, an enticing picture of God, as you will have already picked up. In this view, it is for the people of God to work in harmony with the Spirit, as they

---

[170] Flett, *The Witness of God*, p. 40.
[171] Flett, *The Witness of God*, p. 38.

seek to participate in God's mission as part of an ongoing process, until the climax of history when Christ returns.[172]

Thirdly, at the opposite end of the spectrum to the first view, is the idea that the church is the agent of mission, without God having a part to play in it. This is the view that has prevailed through much of colonial mission history, even before the term *missio Dei* emerged. It is important to note that this view is not specifically Trinitarian, in the sense that the Spirit's role is not as the agent by which God sovereignly leads the church on His mission. It was fit for an age of humanistic philosophy. A sensitive guiding and empowering role for the Spirit of God who leads the church on mission is not included in this traditional programmatic approach. Rather, the church leads mission endeavours, as God's trusted steward. Clearly this may not be termed a fully Trinitarian theology of mission.

The second of Flett's examples is the closest to my view that mission belongs to the Trinity.

Willingen: case example

A crucial turning point regarding the adoption of *missio Dei* theology as a theological label fit for world missionary work occurred at the important Missionary Council that met in Willingen,

---

[172] Flett, *The Witness of God*, p. 38.

Germany in 1952. It was here that *missio Dei* theology started its course towards a fuller expression and development of its ideas. *Missio Dei* was generally accepted as a theological idea at the 1952 International Missionary Council.[173] There was not, as such, clear acceptance of a particular view of what *missio Dei* theology should assume as a model in its first expression. The three models have all had their proponents since the inception of the use of the term.[174] Indeed, this is still the case, although in more recent years the work of the *missio Trinitatis* has become more strongly associated with *missio Dei*.[175] Moreover, there has never been a clearly defined classical model of *missio Dei*, which means that no one of the three models may be considered to be the original view.

Much of what is discussed in the following chapters seeks to develop a Trinitarian picture of God as inviting, welcoming and communicating as a divine family with His erring children. In the case of the second view, the importation of the Trinity as an all-embracing multicultural missionary community finds its most ready connection to *missio Dei*. The church pictures a God who welcomes participation in the Trinity's mission, rather than, on the one hand, the church more or less owning mission until Christ returns, or on the other, the church having nothing to do with God's mission at all until Christ returns.

There is a fourth view, which is entertained as part of a more liberal universalism, exemplified by philosophers such as the late philosopher-theologian John Hick.[176] Universalists argue that there is no grand mission as such, which would be associated with the particularist overtones of Christian missiology, where only those who accept Christ are to be part of God's mission to redeem humankind. Universalists argue that all world religions lead to the

---

173 Flett, *The Witness of God*, p. 55.

174 Flett, *The Witness of God*, pp. 38, 39.

175 Rev Canon Mark Oxbrow, *Trinity and Mission – a review of sources* Pub: Mission Round Table (Occasional Bulletin of OMF Research) Sept 2012 Vol 7 No. 2, p.1; Flett, *The Witness of God*, chapter 3.

176 Charles, M. Cameron, 'John Hick's Religious World', *Evangel* 15.1 (Spring 1997), pp. 22-27.

same goal, seeking to unite humanity to a God who transcends all particular world religions and their versions of god or divinity. In this case, one and all pictures of God, or the divine, are simply roads that lead to the same god. In this sense there is not really a particular missiology that could rightly be called *missio Dei*.

Although universalism is strictly not part of a discussion of *missio Dei* theology, in terms of the Christian tradition generally it does demonstrate a strong postmodern outlook that many people in Western society seriously entertain. Many youth ministers will testify that young people are asking, 'Why can't all religions be seen as valid ways to get to know God?' Students doing youth ministry courses at our college report the same questions being regularly asked by youth among whom they minister.

Although the fourth view has gained popularity among some philosophical theologians as well as popular writers, it was not formally connected to the other three typologies which had closer proximity to Willingen, and the emergence of the idea that God Himself is a missionary being. Of course, universalism has always been one possible interpretation open to theological thought, and there are Christians who argue that in the end everyone will become part of God's eternal world. In this view, it is unthinkable that anyone who gets a chance to meet God face to face could reject Him. Generally speaking, this is not a theological concept that is developed in this book.

Willingen: the *Missio Dei* apologetic

The Council that met at Willingen in 1952 was a kind of watershed moment in terms of the development of a theology regarding the missionary God who embodies His own mission. The introduction of *missio Dei* did no more than provide a general picture of God as a missionary who seeks to reconcile people to Himself. It was of great apologetic importance to missionary agencies and their work among non-Western peoples. Colonialism had included missionary endeavours in the eighteenth, nineteenth and twentieth centuries, as part of its efforts to take Westernised Christian culture to non-

Western nations. The central idea was that the peoples of the cultures outside the West should essentially take on the culture of the Western missionaries who brought the gospel to them.

Western missionaries were increasingly being criticised in the twentieth century, after the Second World War, because of their imposition of the Western culture of Christendom on non-Western, non-Christian nations.[177] This led to accusations of abuse in terms of theft of their precious raw materials and the enforcement of Western culture upon them. By importing the Christendom version of the gospel, colonial powers had denied non-Western peoples the freedom to retain their originating cultures that formed part of their identities.

Western Christian beliefs and practices had been worked out over centuries, and were suited to Western Europeans, but this form of Christendom culture was not suited to many of the non-Western nations that the missionaries sought to convert. Colonialism and the West's cultural Christendom were essentially marriage partners in terms of the type of Christianity that other peoples of the world were meant to embrace if they were to become 'proper' Christians. Cultures other than the European brand were viewed by Western missionaries as being evil and pagan. This was arrogance of the worst kind.

In the 1950s began a strong trend of postcolonial re-evaluation, where colonialism came to be thought of as abusive and corrupt because it had forced its version of Christendom culture on non-Western Christian converts and their societies. It had not helped them to work out how Christianity could work in a way that suited their own cultural contexts. The growing post-colonial critique included judgements against the use of Christianity to win support for the West among native peoples.

This evaluation was taking place in the light of non-Western societies that had a different culture to that of the West, for which the West had not sought to contextualise the gospel. Many non-

---

177 Stanford Encyclopedia of Philosophy, 'Colonialism', May 2006. Available at http://plato.stanford.edu/entries/colonialism/ (accessed 28th October 2015).

Western theologians, church leaders and politicians have continued to react to the prospect of Western missionary agency work in their countries because of the memory of colonial Christendom missionaries who did much to undermine and destroy their native cultures.

An African critique of colonial missionary work

Contemporary African theologians, for example in Nigeria and Kenya, have insisted that Christianity needs to be contextualised. Some important African theologians state this very strongly. Abraham Akrong deconstructs colonial mission as part of his re-contextualisation agenda, where Christian faith needs to be constructed suited to African cultures:

> The emerging issues for post-colonial African missiology is how to de-ideologize and de-imperialize the mission of God in Christ from its colonial and its Eurocentric bondage, which on most occasions did hamper the universal appeal of God's message of salvation in Christ.[178]

We can clearly see that the picture painted by colonial Christendom was a horrifying portrayal of a God who abused people's rights. Reading between the lines, Akrong is challenging the Western picture of God as an imperialistic majesty who approved of the wanton theft of African cultural identity as Western values were forced on African people groups with the aim of deconstructing their own cultural identities. Akrong goes on with a critique of colonialism's missiology that still has a strong influence on some non-Western Christians, looking, as many do, to Europe as

---

[178] Abraham Akrong, 'Deconstructing Colonial Mission – New Missiological Perspective in African Christianity', in Afe Adogame, Gerloff Roswith and Klaus Hock, *Christianity in Africa and the African Diaspora: The Appropriation of a Scattered Heritage,* London: Continuum International Publishing Group (2008), p. 64.

the place where Christianity came from in the colonial period of the Euro-empires. He comments:

> The co-option of the universal symbols of Christianity as a function of colonial empire-building was made possible by the fabrication of an imperial theology based on an exclusive and a narrow interpretation of the Judeo-Christian concept of covenant. In this exclusive and narrow interpretation of covenant, election was understood as a special vocation of Western Christendom in God's economy of salvation. This allowed Western Christendom to develop the idea that it has been elected to spread Christianity and civilize the rest of the world in anticipation of the kingdom of God as, for example, one finds in the nationalistic poems of Kipling. This imperial theology for empire-building led to the mutation and transformation of theological concepts into ideological categories for political domination. The result was the 'domestication' of God's covenant of grace with all humanity in Christ, the 'territorialization' of the kingdom of God, the 'politicization' of evangelism, and the 'imperialization' of the symbol of Christ.[179]

It is not hard to understand how some African diaspora Christians now living in the West do not trust white Western Christians, as they associate them with imperialistic abuse of their originating cultures. This makes it hard for some of them to conceptualise what benefits their communities would obtain by forming partnerships with the white westernised Christians among whom they live. I have deep sympathies with them because cultural memories of the abuse of their homeland cultures is part of their psychology. Akrong rightly challenges Christians in the West about their historical attempts to dissolve differing cultural identities, be it in his own context of African culture (of which there is more than one) or in other non-Western cultures. His challenge is relevant to

---

[179] Akrong, 'Deconstructing Colonial Mission', p. 65.

all of our culture-specific forms of Christianity, in the context of Western multiculturalism. If we do not overcome our own community's ethnocentric ideologies by becoming aware of cultural values other than our own, which are Christianised and on display to our non-Western brothers and sisters, there is little hope that we can form meaningful partnerships with our multicultural brothers and sisters living in the West.

How Willingen offered impetus to a new way of engaging in God's mission

We must thank Akrong for this critique. In terms of the multicultural Trinity, the challenge reverses: the need is for all the cultures that form our pluralistic Western society to maintain their identities, but at the same time to partner and learn from each other's perspectives as we seek to unite as brothers and sisters of the same heavenly family. This contemporary critique offers an insight into the need to non-domesticate 'God's covenant of grace' from a 'narrow [cultural] interpretation', which was part of the imperialistic theology of Christendom missiology. The Protestant version of Western Christendom, which was essentially equated to be God's chosen vehicle for the acculturation of non-Western converts, was already forming as an accusation against the work of missionaries from the West by the time of the Protestant Council meeting at Willingen in 1952. *Missio Dei* theology became part of the apologetic to de-imperialise the 'narrow' concept of missionary work outside of the West. God was outside culture, and He incarnated in various cultures by the Spirit of Christ. This incarnational work of the Spirit was envisioned to help people in those cultures to shape their expressions of Christianity in ways that suited their own cultures.

Missio Dei apologetics firmly opens God's mission to include a broader view of God as Trinity, who seeks to help different cultural groups think through how they want to express the Christian faith in ways appropriate to their own cultural context. This includes guidance to help multicultural ethnic groups form identities suited to their new lives in the Western context. From this point of view, the introduction of the apologetic concept that has mission belonging to God, rather than belonging to Western Christendom missionary imperialism, began the liberation process that would lead to a better appreciation of God's activity in mission by the work of His Spirit.

Rather than imperialistic takeover bids of non-Western cultures, Christianity needed to be acculturated to suit the various cultures it engaged. This is no less the case in the context of Western multiculturalism and pluralism. One aspect of pluralism is religious pluralism, in the form of world religions coming to the West along with migrants. Karkkainen offers a vital insight to help multicultural missional churches work with people of different faiths. He focuses our attention on the diversity implied by the three persons in the Trinity, set in the context of Their unity of being, purpose and love. I argue that the vision of the social Trinity, new as the postmodern idea is compared to its historical tradition-based conception (see chapter 7), provides an important picture of God the Trinity as one that seeks to welcome those from other faiths into dialogue and conversation with MT-shaped Christian communities.[180]

This is what the picture of God as a multicultural Trinity family provides for us, to inform new kinds of multi-ethnic churches, or partnerships, between different cultural groups. Of course, MT theology does not seek to force the need to plant multi-ethnic or multicultural churches. People of a given culture can start to live out their Christian lives in a way that is appropriate for their own peculiar circumstances as Christian beliefs are reinterpreted for a new Western multicultural situation. Moreover, Christian Indians will be better placed to engage in mission with Hindus, for example, compared to Christians of other nationalities. Akrong is not arguing against the possibility of partnerships of African Christians with other ethnic groups living in the West, per se. His deconstruction of

---

[180] Veli-Matti Karkkainen, *Trinity and Religious Pluralism: The Doctrine of the Trinity in Christian Theology of Religions,* Aldershot: Ashgate (2004), pp. 1-12.

imperialistic views of God challenge contemporary Westernised churches to think carefully about what they assume new converts from another cultural group, living in the West, should take on from their own culturally determined outlooks if meaningful partnerships are to take place.

The apologetic idea of *missio Dei* that Hartenstein formulated has over time come to provide ever more fully a way for missiology to escape imprisonment by any given cultural expression of Christianity. All of our multicultural expressions of faith can become part of a celebration of all peoples who may worship in multicultural gatherings from time to time. If we were to begin to model the all-inclusive multicultural united family of God to our societies, then larger multicultural Christian gatherings would be an amazing way of saying to broader society, 'Look what our God is like. Look at what belonging to His multicultural family means.' Of course, we will never be able to manufacture multicultural churches into being. These kinds of communities cannot come into being unless peoples feel called together to form such missional communities.

Imagine and reflect

Imagine what it would look like if you had the opportunity to help organise a multicultural social event, where each Christian cultural group living in your region would come in traditional dress and could offer tasters of their favourite foods, in order for Christians to intentionally get to know each other better.

- What would you like to see at such an event?

- How many different cultural groups could you invite?

- What would you like their stalls to include?

- What kind of social activities would you provide to enable people to mingle and get to know each other better?

- What sensitivities would you need to take into account when planning this event with your team? For example, in some Black churches men and women are separated in worship services: men on one side, women on the other.

Take some time to jot down your ideas. Then take some time to reflect with others, and learn from each other's ideas. Why not take some time to intentionally pray for the guidance of the MT for how some of these ideas could become a reality in your locality? The important question to consider is whether or not you discern that God is calling people to participate in this kind of venture together?

Father, Son and Holy Spirit welcome your missional imagination and ideas. Join with the Spirit of creation and re-creation in imagining new ways of being the people of God together into being.

Missio Dei as Trinitarian: Lesslie Newbigin

Bishop Lesslie Newbigin brought an important emphasis to the Trinity in *missio Dei* theological thinking. He had his own starting point for *missio Dei*, which he framed specifically in Trinitarian terms.[181] Newbigin's own ideas drew together the traditional view,

---

[181] Newbigin, *The Open Secret*, chapters 4, 5.

where mission belongs to the church, with the view that the Spirit needs to be liberated from domestication to doctrines in order to lead the church to participate in God's mission.[182] In his classic treatment of missional theology, *The Open Secret: An Introduction to the Theology of Mission*, he founded his missiology on an open view of the Trinity, where the Father sends the Son and then the Spirit to reconcile and unite all peoples together in the kingdom of God. God is portrayed to be active in the historical processes reconciling all peoples into the Trinitarian family. Newbigin's open view allowed for the self-revelatory Trinity to reveal the *missio Dei* to its peoples through ongoing prophetic discernment of the *missio Trinitatis*. Newbigin propounded his version of Trinitarianism in three propositions.

Firstly, he spoke of God's mission as the proclamation of God's 'kingship' over 'all human history' and the 'whole cosmos'.[183] Mission has to do with the completion of God's mission to universally unite all peoples and cultures to Himself in Christ.[184] In this first sense, the invisible Father is pictured as the source of all authority who invites and welcomes us into the kingdom.

Secondly, he posited mission to be the 'presence' of God and His 'kingship in Jesus and the church.'[185] Newbigin's missiology particularised and limited mission in the sense that it was to be located in Christ as its specific agent, and in the church as the sphere through which God is at work. In this regard it sounds like Newbigin was a proponent of the traditional view, to the extent that the church was the proper place for people to come once they were converted. I much prefer to talk of people becoming part of a Christian community, because to many postmodern peoples the word 'church' implies a place that is lifeless and irrelevant to their lives.

---

[182] Newbigin, *The Open Secret*, pp. 53-58.

[183] Newbigin, *The Open Secret*, chapter 5.

[184] Newbigin, *The Open Secret*, p. 56.

[185] Newbigin, *The Open Secret*, p. 56.

Thirdly, Newbigin argued that *missio Dei* is based on the guidance of the Spirit who enables the church to discern what God is already doing among non-believers outside the church to prepare the ground for further mission among those as yet not reached by the gospel, as much as it was a work of the Spirit with people within the church. By this Newbigin meant that the church did not own or control the work of the Spirit of Christ controlling where the Spirit was at work in society outside the church. The people of God always need to seek to participate in the Trinity's mission with those in society who do not as yet have a faith in God:

> I have affirmed that God's kingship is present in the church; but it must be insisted that it is not the property of the church. It is not domesticated within the church. Mission is not simply the self-propagation of the church by putting forth the power that inheres in its life. To accept that picture would be to sanction an appalling distortion of mission. On the contrary, the active agent of mission is a power that rules, guides, and goes before the church: the free, sovereign, living power of the Spirit of God. Mission is not just something that the church does; it is something that is done by the Spirit, who is himself the witness, who changes both the world and the church, who always goes before the church in its missionary journey.[186]

In this rather neat summation, Newbigin embraced a 'both/and' view of *missio Dei*. Simply stated, he implied a spiritual theology of *missio Dei* through which the Christian community needs to discern the work of God's Spirit ahead of it in the world. The Spirit is at work ahead of the church calling God's missionary people to follow Christ as He continues His mission in secular society to which they are invited to participate with Him. Mission belongs to the Trinity, not to the church. The church is not in charge of the Trinity's mission. The church is called to participate in it. More importantly for the present discussion, Newbigin framed a foundational

---

[186] Newbigin, *The Open Secret*, p. 56.

principle for why it is important for missional theology to embrace a Trinitarian view of God's work in the world, in which the church can participate. Our participation in *missio Dei* has a goal, which is eschatological in nature: it has to do with the arrival of the eschatological kingdom of God as a full earthly reality.

The future hope of the eschatological unification of all things with God, at the end of the age, is projected backwards by Jesus' end-time parables, towards God's people in the present, so that they can shape their faith on the hope of the future kingdom.[187] The future kingdom pictures all peoples united around the throne of God (see Revelation 7). The goal is to have peoples of the world ready to participate in this eternal new order. The following diagram explains how teaching about the future eternal kingdom informs the church today.

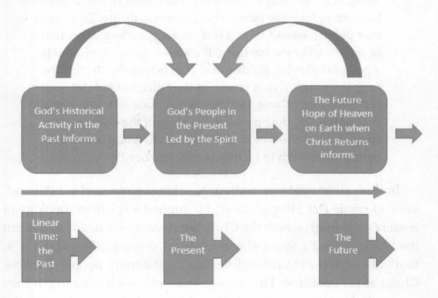

This diagram shows that the parables and stories in the Bible, which tell us about the peace and joy of the future kingdom of glory,

---

[187] Tom Sine, *The New Conspirators: Creating the Future One Mustard Seed at a Time*, Downers Grove: IVP Books (2008), pp. 110-128.

were told by Jesus so that we might start to seek to live out our lives as multicultural communities, visibly in the midst of a divided multicultural pluralistic Western society. The future descriptions of the kingdom finally established, in Christ's parables and the book of Revelation, are provided so that contemporary believers can critically reflect on what they are to become in the future age. Views of the future age help us to reflect on our own lives now and in turn to then seek to jettison unholy thoughts and behaviours to embrace the visions of the holy people of God portrayed in the future kingdom eschatologically realised.

We can also talk of the historical ascension of Jesus back to His Father in heaven.[188] Pentecost began the Spirit's missional work in the world and the trajectory of history towards a new world order. In this three-part description of the Trinity's mission to reconcile all peoples to Godself, the ascended Jesus has overcome sin, death and damnation by dying for the sins of humankind and rising again. Christ is also our example to follow as we reflect on His life, deeds and teachings found in the gospels. His position at God's right hand means that the power of evil may be overcome in the name of the all-powerful Christ. Of course, evil will not be fully overthrown until Christ returns. The multicultural people of God, and the peoples of the world, live in the continuing reality of Pentecost, where the Spirit of God brings about the reconciliation and transformation of believers in the name of Christ.

Parousia means 'presence'. It refers to the in-breaking of the reign of God, as a final reality for all to enjoy at the climax of history, when Christ is once again revealed to the cosmos in all His majestic glory and brings about its renewal. It also is an emergent process portrayed by God's people living together in unity in Christian communities. These communities provide a picture of God's kingdom of love to faith-seekers in action. Their community fellowship is the hermeneutic of the gospel as Newbigin so aptly phrased it, acting as a foretaste of the future kingdom to faith-

---

[188] Acts 1:9-11.

seekers.[189] The word pictures of Revelation envision the time of the *Parousia*, where a multitude made up of all tongues, peoples and nations gather around God's throne worshipping Godself together.[190]

These three acts of the coming of Christ, sent by the Father, informed Newbigin's missiology. Newbigin looked forward to the consummation of all things, with Christ's second coming being the climax of *missio Dei*. He remains an important voice connected to the development of a practical *missio Dei* theology, which locates the Trinity as a very appropriate part of its deep values and convictions.

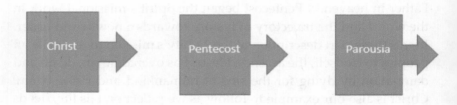

Conclusion: teleological research methodology based on Trinitarian epistemology

As professional missional practical theologians engage in mission, they do so based on the conviction that the invisible Father sent the Son to incarnate in human history. God in Christ has made humanity part of God's story and life. The Spirit of Christ continues the mission of Jesus in the world. Hence my *missio Trinitatis* MT theology sets the methodology of missional practical theology in the context of a God who reveals Himself through Scripture, anointed reason, experiences and prophetic discernment of what God is doing in society. The incarnate Creator of the cosmos in Christ is still at work in the world, leading it to the telos of new creation. Hence when *missio Trinitatis* practical theologians seek to research and discern what the *missio Dei* is at work in a particular

---

[189] Newbigin, *The Gospel in a Pluralistic Society*, chapter 18.
[190] Revelation 7.

community, it is done based on the deep conviction that God reveals Himself in the material world and the relationships that occur among ordinary men and women. My missional practical theology methodology is based on the conviction that the social Trinity reveals Itself to human beings because Father, Son and Spirit do so based on their interpersonal life shared as three persons who are one being.

Each of the persons in the divine economy has a part to play in the sending mission that defines God's family, as inclusive of all who want to meaningfully become part of it. *Missio Dei* theology needs a Trinitarian foundation, because only a relational deity that is socially and relationally active in the world can properly guide the people of God to engage in God's mission.[191] Newbigin did not, as such, come up with the idea of the metaphor of the Trinity as a multicultural missional family. I am not aware of anyone else using this metaphor in quite the way I have here in the context of my *missio Trinitatis* practical missional theology. The teleological eschatology of Parousia forms the overall purposive direction practical missional theologians aim to reach because we have the single magnificent goal of the eternal kingdom of God coming on earth as it is in heaven, in which all peoples and cultures will share life together as a diverse united people for evermore.

---

[191] Stanley J. Grenz, *Rediscovering The Triune God: The Trinity in Contemporary Theology*, Minneapolis: Fortress Press, (2004), pp. 117-118.

Chapter 7
Pastiches of the Trinity in modern and contemporary theological thought

In this chapter we will seek to enhance our understanding of the missionary God's nature. In order to formulate a good basis of a pragmatic practical missional theology and methodology suitable to discern the Trinity's mission, where all followers of Christ are presently part of the Father's kingdom community, it is important to draw on the theological insights of several of the major Trinitarian theologians of the twentieth and twenty-first centuries. These theologians have done much to help us appreciate why it is so important for us to understand the Trinity as part of our epistemological missional practical theology and methodology. MT theology also makes God's people participants in God's mission to welcome new peoples into the Trinity's eternal family as part of the *missio Trinitatis*. When I talk of the Trinity as a family I am also speaking metaphorically in a certain sense because it is an analogy to human families. Analogic reasoning is not used to make exact scientific claims about God's nature and being in theology, or, of course, how we might go about researching potential new communities to discern the *missio Dei* among differing peoples and communities.

I have developed much of my thinking about the Trinity's mission with reference to the theologians Karl Barth,[192] Karl

---

[192] Barth, *Church Dogmatics*, Vol. 1.1.

Rahner,[193] John Zizioulas,[194] Jurgen Moltmann[195] and the more recent contributions of the psycho-social practical pastoral theology of Peter Holmes,[196] among others. In this chapter we cannot hope to do justice to their works beyond taking key highlights from each of their theologies of the Trinity. Holmes provides a suggestive methodical approach for work among people to discern God's work in people's lives by enabling people to hear God's voice for themselves. This obviously requires a belief and conviction that God can really communicate with people. This requires an open view of the universe into which God can communicate with people on an intuitive level. Evidence of this suggestively occurring has been found in studies done of a phenomenological type.[197] These snapshots will offer helpful insights that can be utilised in a practical missional theology, which can help our Christian communities enhance their picture of the MT.

Trinity is the family to which we all belong. I suggest it needs to shape the projections of our Christian community personas to those who view them from the outside, as they get to know us better. It will be the loving and sacrificial words and deeds of each follower of Christ that will provide a practical picture of what God's love feels like when it is received by faith-seekers from human agents.

---

[193] Karl Rahner, *The Trinity*, Translated by Donceel Joseph, New York: Herder and Herder, (1986).

[194] John D. Zizioulas, *The Eucharistic Communion and the World*, London: T & T Clark, (2011); John D. Zizioulas, *Being as Communion*, London: Darton Longman and Todd, (2013).

[195] Jurgen Moltmann, *The Crucified God*, London: SCM Press (2008). Jurgen Moltmann, *The Trinity and the Kingdom of God*, London: SCM Press, (1981).

[196] Holmes, Trinity in Human Community Exploring Congregational Life in the Image of the Social Trinity. Peter R. Holmes, and Susan B. Williams, Susan, *Becoming More Like Christ A Contemporary Biblical Journey*, London: Paternoster (2007).

[197] Andrew, R. Hardy, 'Spiritual and Missional Philosophical Theology', (2012), Doctoral Thesis Chapter3. Available at: https://www.academia.edu/2416319/Mission_and_Spirituality (accessed 30th November 2015).

Discussion in this chapter has been balanced to offer foundational insights that some readers will not want to explore at a deeper technical level.[198] The aim is to produce a short introduction to a practical theology of *missio Trinitatis*, as part of the picture of the God who has a mission to reconcile all peoples into the eternal family. MT theology is also part of the thinking behind this chapter and its methodological epistemology.

To conclude the chapter I will draw together the key ideas of our five theologians and create my own pastiche which will help us to better understand the basis of my MT theology. The term 'pastiche' fits well with my own attraction to the creative openings that postmodern philosophy offers to those of us who believe that it partly offers a window to re-engage with mystery in the sight of the infinite God whom Christians trust.

Karl Barth (1886–1968): The self-revelation of the Trinity

Karl Barth never used the Latin terms *missio Dei* or *missio Trinitatis*. In Barth's theology, God is in the first place God in action (*actio Dei*), because He sent His Son to reveal God to the world.[199] This God was in action through His Word recorded in Scripture, and in His self-revelation in the life, death, resurrection and ascension of Jesus Christ.[200] The incarnation of the Son of God sets Barth's theology of the Trinity in the context of a historical revelation of the invisible Father, who sent His Son to redeem the world and to provide a picture of God to humanity through His life, teachings and deeds.[201] In other words, Barth's Christology opens up an understanding of the Father, Son and Spirit to humanity, because Jesus reveals God

---

[198] However, if what we consider in the next few pages stimulates some readers to consult more formal works, which offer critical reviews of these thinker's ideas, a good work to consult is. Veli-Matti Karkkainen, *The Trinity Global Perspectives*, Louisville: Westminster John Know Press (2007).

[199] Karl Barth, *God in Action*, New York: Round Table Press (1963), pp. 11,12

[200] Barth, *God in Action*.

[201] Barth, *Church Dogmatics*, Vol. 1.1, pp. 399-414.

to the world.[202] In the divine ordering of the economy of God, the Son is sent by the Father to potentially reunite humankind to the Father's family.[203]

Even though Barth never used the term *missio Dei*, it is clearly appropriate to include his theology in a consideration of a picture of the missionary God which is framed around the doctrine of the Trinity. This is because Barth's theology of the self-revelation of God shows how it is vital to understand God's love-motivated action in sending Jesus to a fallen world.

In Barth's theology of the Trinity, the source of God's self-revelation is through the Word of God and Christ the Word (the Bible).[204] The Holy Spirit enters Barth's theology as the Spirit of Christ.[205] But the Spirit is also its own person as well, as Lord in its own right in the Trinity.[206]

It is Christ and the Father who send the Spirit, after Jesus returns to the Father.[207] The fundamental Trinitarian formula in Barth is that 'God reveals himself. He reveals himself through himself. He reveals himself.'[208] Barth was keen to emphasise that God, in His self-revelation, made it possible for human beings to know Him.[209] Because God puts His self-revelation into human language, through the Word and the God-man (Christ), He has made Himself known to humanity. The Scriptures convey the canonical revelation of God in Christ to His church throughout the ages. A key question is, to what extent is the Word of God revelation?

In classical philosophical terms, we might ask, 'Can God ever be known if He is completely different to the human creatures He has made?' Barth did much to address this question, which is often asked by those who do not believe that it is possible for human

---

202 Barth, *Church Dogmatics*, Vol. 1.1, p. 424.

203 Barth, *Church Dogmatics*, Vol. 1.1, p. 451.

204 Karkkainen, *The Trinity*, p. 72.

205 Barth, *Church Dogmatics*, Vol. 1.1, p. 452.

206 Barth, *Church Dogmatics*, Vol. 1.1, pp. 450-452.

207 Karl Barth, *Church Dogmatics*.

208 Barth, *Church Dogmatics*, Vol. 1.1, p. 296.

209 Barth, *Church Dogmatics*, Vol. 1.2, pp. 362-371.

beings to understand an ineffable being. To understand God would make us God. There is no place in this view, therefore, for us to be able to discern God's mission, or to participate in it alongside God. In this understanding, God seems distant and uninterested in His people. Once He has saved them He leaves them to the care of the church.

This presents an appalling picture of God. God seems to be uninterested in His people once they are safely in His fishing net. It is essentially a non-Trinitarian view. We are asking, remember, whether God can be subjectively or objectively understood in any meaningful way by finite creatures. How Barth answers this question is important for a theology of *missio Trinitatis*, where God's people can know what He is like and what He is guiding them to do, so they can join Him in communicating the gospel to a lost world.

The theologian Veli-Matti Karkkainen asks:

> How can the human being know God in any way? Doesn't that make God an object, like other objects to be observed? Barth's response is a qualified yes. This means that God is an 'object' only to the extent that he gives himself to us to be known. God 'gives himself to man in His Word as a real object.' God is object by his own grace, from his own initiative, in his sovereign freedom. A related question is, if so, could human words ever reach to the level of speaking about God? Here again, Barth gives a qualified yes. Human words can only be used to speak of the transcendent God to the extent God 'elevates' our words to their proper use, this giving them truth.'[210]

We must remember that Barth was coming from the Protestant angle, which primarily limited the self-revelation of God to Christ, the Scriptures and the sacraments. Hence what can be known of God is to be found in these symbolic, word-based revelatory media. Barth did not apply his theology of the God who can be known

---

[210] Karkkainen, *The Trinity*, p. 68.

through Christ and the Word to a Spirit-sensitive view, where the Spirit may be said to prophetically lead the church on God's mission in the contemporary post-apostolic setting. He clearly believed the Spirit convicts Christians of sin and the need to live a righteous life. He limited the work of the Spirit to the framework of the Bible, the church and the sacraments – he was no charismatic. However, the breakthrough in Barth's Trinitarian theology is that God is in action through His self-revelation.

More importantly, Barth's contribution to future developments in Trinitarian theology is in his argument that God brought Himself into human history through the Son.[211] The words and deeds of Jesus are all part of the records in the gospels of God's self-revelation through Christ. We can obtain a picture of God from Christ.

The incarnation of the Son of God is an event in God's own being. God enters the world through His Son. God journeys in the Son throughout His life, death, resurrection and ascension, engaging with real people in the real world. The Father sends the Son to gather the Father's elect ones. The Son is sent to bring about their reconciliation.[212] By so doing, God enters human history and thus He can be known through His historical self-manifestation. Karkkainen captures the significance of Barth's theology well:

> Not only are the roles of the Father and Son different in
> the sphere of election and reconciliation, but history is also
> being incorporated into the divine being.[213]

This historicisation of the Son in human history is a vital step in the development of a Trinitarian practical theology, as it means that God engages in the historical processes of mission in which the church participates alongside Christ. Beyond this point, Barth does not develop a spiritual theology which can help us think through how to discern the guidance of the Spirit of Christ, and which may

---

[211] Barth, *Church Dogmatics*, Vol. 1.2, pp. 45-70.
[212] Barth, *Church Dogmatics*, Vol. 1.1, pp. 399-413.
[213] Karkkainen, *The Trinity*, p. 73.

be said to make God's mission known to His people. What Barth offers are three important building blocks for a practical theology of *missio Trinitatis*.

Firstly, he provides a theology of the self-revelation of the Trinity. Secondly, he develops a theology of a God who can be known for who He really is, because God has sovereignly elected to make Himself known in human language, through the historical theological records of the life of Jesus. Thirdly, God was, and is, active in the historical processes of the world, which means His will for the world is made known to humans through the incarnation, based on His self-revelation in Christ and the Word of God.

All three points are important for a theology of *missio Trinitatis*. Barth's views help us to form the picture of the Trinity that revealed itself intentionally through Christ and the Word.

We need to move on to see how other thinkers have built on Barth's paradigm-shifting theology of God.

Karl Rahner (1904–1984): The economic and imminent Trinity and salvation history

Rahner's Trinitarian theology was practical in its aims, just as Barth's was. Like Barth, Rahner believed that leaving the Trinity to the pages of philosophical theology would be of no practical theological value to the church. I would further add that the doctrine of the Trinity is of no use to *missio Dei* theology if it is hived off into an intellectual theological sub-discipline for academics to muse on alone in their ivory towers.

Rahner reacted against earlier classical views of the Trinity, which rendered the Trinity an afterthought to theology (the German theologian Schleiermacher did this in his dogmatic theology). This lack of a Trinitarian theology came to heavily influence the discipline of systematic theology in the West, which many university theology courses still hold to. Indeed, Karkkainen points out that the unity of the one God (monotheism) had all but eclipsed the doctrine of the Trinity in Western theology up until the beginning of the twentieth century. This was because of the focus on a philosophical idea of God that made Him impersonal and inactive in the world (i.e. Deism). According to Karkkainen, Rahner had three concerns about the over-emphasis of the one being of God in the technical theology of the West, to the detriment of the three persons in the Trinity.

Firstly, Rahner was concerned that the emphasis on the oneness of God, accompanied by the failure to develop the threeness of the Godhead, made it look as 'if everything which matters for us in God has already been said'.[214] In other words, the unity of God took the upper hand over the threeness.[215] Therefore, there was not a place for further investigation into the threeness, as the oneness had become the heart of Western theology's view of God. In other words, it is impossible to really know a sole, isolated, infinitely incomprehensible God. Strictly speaking, all references to the Trinity could be removed from Western dogmatic theology without substantively changing its doctrine of God. This one God was essentially non-relational, for all practical purposes, in the real world of human interpersonal life. This God was also radically deconstructed by very liberal New Testament theologians, such as Rudolf Bultmann, making Jesus a myth who never really did or said the things the gospels record. Rahner did not agree with Bultmann. In his view, the church needed to return to the Jesus described in the Bible as the real revelation of a personal and accessible God, whom Jesus taught His followers to call Father.

Secondly, Rahner critiqued the classical view of the pre-eminence of the unity of God, at the expense of not recognising the particular differences among the persons of the Trinity.[216] The danger was that the Trinity, including the incarnation of the Son, become abstract themes set in systematic philosophical theology, without recognition of a real personalistic view of Father, Son or Spirit, as the dynamic personal relational God that the Bible portrays.

---

[214] Rahner, *The Trinity*, p. 17.
[215] Karkkainen, *The Trinity*, p. 77.
[216] Karkkainen, *The Trinity*, p. 77.

Thirdly, Rahner argued that philosophical discussion of the Trinity makes it a matter of abstract, non-substantive thought. It separates the revelation of the persons of God from human history. The real incarnate Son of God, represented through the life of Christ, turns into theological smoke that blows away if the Jesus of history cannot be known, as scholars like Bultmann claimed He could not be. After all, speculative abstractions about God cannot be made concrete in the real lives of people of faith if Christ cannot be known as our historical saviour.

On this final point, Rahner is close to Barth, by bringing human history into the Son of God. What Rahner achieved was to bring the Trinity to the foreground, as Barth did, because the persons of the Trinity are revealed in substantive terms through the incarnation of the Son in human history.[217] The gospels need to be taken as real records of what Jesus did and said, as well as authentic records of what the early church believed to be the verified truth about Jesus' life and teachings. This need not imply that critical theological questions cannot be applied to scientific study of the Scriptures, of course. However, we need to return to the Jesus portrayed in the gospels to inform our theological reflections.

My phraseology of 'returning to Jesus' has been radically challenged by contemporary scholars, such as Dale Allison. I have given my views in chapter 2 on how I see the reality of the Jesus whose words and works were recorded in the gospels.

We have already noticed that each gospel writer portrayed a particular picture of Christ to his audience, but this does not mean that the accounts were not based on the resurrected new life of the Lord, of whom Paul said at least 500 eyewitnesses to His resurrection were still living in his lifetime.[218] The starting point of Rahner's Trinitarian theology is somewhat premodern in its assumptions, with a personal God who can be known through His manifestation in salvation history. God is to be related to as 'our

---

[217] Rahner, *The Trinity*, pp. 24-33.
[218] 1 Corinthians 15:6.

Father'. Christ is our brother who empathises with our human condition and frailties.[219]

This is where we meet Rahner's famous rule:

> The 'economic' Trinity is the 'immanent' Trinity and the 'immanent' Trinity is the 'economic' Trinity.[220]

He agrees, in essence, with Barth here, to the extent that he claims that God's inner hidden mysterious life (imminent shared life of the persons of the Trinity) has been revealed by God in the sending of the Son and the Spirit (as part of God's economy that administers His saving presence in the world of history). Therefore, to know the God revealed through the Son is to really know the Trinity in terms of character and nature (I argue by this that we obtain a picture of God as a family). There is no second, hidden ineffable Trinity behind the mask of a theologically constructed Trinity, in other words. The God known through the Son is the God who has made Himself known, and none other than God Himself is really known as Father Son and Spirit, revealed to real people by the real Jesus now seated with His Father in Heaven as Jesus Christ the Lord.

God enters into human history through the Son of God. This means that history, as in Barth, is taken up into the life of God when the God-man returns to heaven. However, in Rahner's view, human history was only taken into Jesus Christ the God-man rather than into the Trinity. He did this to protect the divine transcendence from having mutable humanity becoming part of the Trinity. This seems to undermine his rule, although in Rahner's view it did not undermine it because God could be known through the Son: hence the imminent Trinity is made known by the translation of the Son of God into a human creature.[221] In Rahner's way of thinking, knowing God is not the same as being taken into God's ontological interior life as Father, Son and Spirit.

---

[219] Hebrews 2:14-18.
[220] Rahner, *The Trinity*, p. 22.
[221] John 1:14, 18.

163

Moreover, Rahner believed that the Son of God's becoming human, in a special sense, meant that God's immutable nature was impacted by the incarnation. By the Son taking on human flesh, He engaged in the process of becoming, in the context of the space–time world and in terms of human history, just as a finite mutable human does. The Son becoming the God-man leads to followers of Christ themselves being transformed in salvation history into His likeness. Through the Spirit of the historical Christ, Christians participate in His transformative presence, which enables them to become more like Christ every day, in a process of transformation from one degree of glory to another, as the apostle Paul classically articulated it.[222]

At this point the philosophical theological argument can be left for the reader to follow up in Rahner's own work, if she or he wishes.[223] The important contribution that Rahner makes to a practical missional theology is that the Son's incarnation is a real part of God's coming alongside His people in salvation history. This incarnational historicisation of the Son provides practical theology with a meaningful connection to the real, personal, knowable God-man. The Son, as the God-man sent by the Father, can be known on a historical and relational level by real people in real-life situations.

This is also important to contextual theology, because the Trinity seeks to make itself known in the real-life contexts of humans. Our personal God and Father can be translated into human life because the God-man has taken human historical life up into heaven, which enables each of us, according to Paul, to be spiritually seated at the right hand of Christ in heaven.[224] We need this kind of thinking to be part of a practical missional theology, where the God-man has transported each of us into the eternal life of the Trinity's cosmic family. We are already securely seated in heaven alongside the Son of God as a spiritual reality, according to the apostle Paul.[225]

---

[222] 2 Corinthians 3:18.
[223] Rahner, *The Trinity*.
[224] Ephesians 2:6.
[225] Ephesians 2:6.

164

In terms of my practical theology of *missio Trinitatis*, Rahner's theology of the Son of God is important because it has God meaningfully participate in human history. It provides the possibility for a more intimate knowing of the Son through the indwelling Spirit of Christ. The God-man in heaven understands my real human challenges, and He can help me through His Spirit's presence to overcome challenges I face because He knew similar challenges and overcame them too.

The question of how practical missional theologians may enter into intimate fellowship with Christ will be the subject of chapter 9. What it is important to take from Rahner's Trinitarian theology is his deep respect for the God who has made Himself known, while seeking to maintain the unity of the Trinity, who will never be subject to change in terms of Their eternal nature of love.

For Rahner, the Trinity remains immutable. It is intriguing that the incarnation of the Son potentially implies that He was not immutable during His earthly pilgrimage. However, the Philippians passage which speaks of the Son's decision to empty Himself of His rightful divinity prior to the incarnation seems to make this a self-limitation 'that is removed after the resurrection.'[226] If this is the correct interpretation of the kenotic passage in Philippians, it sits well with Rahner's desire to protect the Holy Trinity from losing its immutability in terms of its divine being becoming inclusive of mutable human nature.

The picture of God portrayed by Rahner is one of the Father, Son and Holy Spirit deeply concerned to empathise with our human condition, as well as desiring each of us to become part of Their eternal family, where our finite beings will no longer be overpowered by evil and sinful motivations, but transformed by Christ's perfect being.

---

[226] Philippians 2:5-8.

John Zizioulas: persons defined by communion

John Zizioulas' theology of communion with God, which comes from his reflections on the persons of the Trinity in relationship to the church and its life, are significant to the development of my theological picture of God. I find his theological voice to be refreshing, coming as it does from the Greek Orthodox Christian tradition. Having been raised in a secular, individualist British culture, I have been positively challenged to seek to grow beyond my individualistic mindset towards what Zizioulas speaks of as persons who exist in communion with other persons in the human and divine family.

I mention these rather personal thoughts because I believe Zizioulas' vision of the Trinity is vital to help people in our individualistic postmodern society discover another way of being, which is part of the Greek Orthodox view of the Trinitarian faith. I do no more at this stage than highlight its importance to a proper missional theology of the church, and the picture of God which our various denominations hold. I believe that in order for our Christian communities to become truly loving, caring and welcoming places, they need to be based on what is known as the social doctrine of the Trinity (which Zizioulas does not take to the extremes of process theology's concept of the social Trinity).

The picture of God held by Orthodox Christians is of persons who are never alone. This means that the persons of God and His people belong to one another, because they share life together in deep fellowship and interpersonal relations through Christ, the mediator of a new covenant of which Christ is eternal High Priest – representing humanity in heaven before the heavenly court.[227] Zizioulas' communion theology, which we are about to consider, is an important part of a contextual framing narrative for the multicultural missional church in the West to learn from. Indeed, we need to ensure that our pictures of God allow for the deeper fellowship with God and one another provided by the social doctrine of the Trinity, or we will be in danger of not authentically

---

[227] Hebrews 9:11-22.

experiencing what it means to live together in intimacy within God's family.

An important work, where Zizioulas develops his theology of communion, is in his monograph, *Being as Communion: Studies in Personhood and Communion*.[228] Essential to his thesis is the profound insight that there is no conscious being without communion. Persons only exist in relationship to other persons, and to God's person as the people of God. An individual does not exist unless he or she exists in relationship to other persons. By being in relationship to other persons, a person comes to know themselves in distinction from the other.

This means it is vital to live in deep, meaningful relationships with other persons, in order to really thrive as persons made in the Trinity's image and likeness. Imagine what it would have been like if as soon as you were born you had been locked up in a dark room, on your own. How could you ever come to know yourself, be able to distinguish yourself from others, or for that matter communicate with others using meaningful language, without any opportunities to interact with even your parents? In some famous cases where children have been locked away in rooms with little human contact for a number of years, they emerge unable to relate to other human beings. They cannot speak, nor can they learn to speak in semantically meaningful sentences. They do not understand what it is to be embraced and they find it impossible to give or receive love and affection from others.

Zizioulas suggests that God designed humanity in the Trinity's image as social relational beings. We do not exist as real selves without other real selves to interact with. We cannot have real conscious awareness of ourselves, as separate selves, if we are isolated from others. Greek Orthodox theology is based on this Trinitarian insight. We all need each other in order to be real persons in our own right. We cannot experience God's love, or human love, if we do not receive it and give it through real actions and words exchanged with others. The church cannot expect faith-

---

[228] Zizioulas, *Being as Communion*.

167

seekers to come to its meetings if there is no meaningful way of forming friendships that matter outside church meetings. The picture Christ portrayed of His Father came through His living and suffering alongside people He helped practically: it was a picture of the Father's heart of love in action to people in the real world.

Zizioulas begins with the church as the place where these kinds of relationships need to exist. The Trinity, as icon of the Greek Orthodox Church, is what Western multicultural churches could learn from. Multi-ethnic churches have already been planted, representing a picture of the God who welcomes all nations and cultures.[229] Our fellowship with people outside of our own groups needs to be inclusive, including friendships with others different to ourselves. We need to identify ourselves in new ways which express inclusivity and welcome of differences in our communities. This calls for maturity, and is what it means to become united as all nations and peoples in Christ. This view of the Trinity is essential to my theology of MT. Karkkainen offers an excellent summary of how Zizioulas conceives this:

> By being a member of the church, a human being becomes an 'image of God,' existing as God Himself exists; he or she takes on God's 'way of being.' 'This way of being ... is a way of relationship with the world, with other people and with God, an event of communion, and that is why it cannot be realized as the achievement of an individual, but only as an ecclesial fact.'[230]

Put in simpler terms, a person does not exist unless they live in relationship with God and other persons. The human being is, therefore, only truly a human being if she or he lives in relationship with other human beings, living out the *imago Trinitatis*. Zizioulas takes this profound starting point for his understanding of the Trinity. Firstly, it comes from the revolutionary idea of the Cappadocian fathers, who identified the essence of the Trinity to be

---

229 F. Scott Spencer, *Journeying through Acts.*
230 Karkkainen, *The Trinity*, pp. 90, 91.

168

persons defined by relations with their counterparts. God's being as Father, Son and Holy Spirit can only remain consciously and ontologically meaningful if the eternal three live in a relationship together, as persons defined by their intra-Trinitarian communion, where each person transparently shares the whole of Themselves with Their counterparts.

Secondly, Zizioulas speaks of this as *koinonia* (Greek word meaning 'things held in common among people of a community').[231] In other words, the Trinity can only exist as three persons united in the one divine being. Their inner *koinonia* also causes Them to share in *koinonia* with those They have created in Their image. The Trinity ecstatically extend Themselves outwards towards others, which defines Their and our participation in Their family, sharing life as sons and daughters of God and as brothers and sisters of Christ. This is how we all can meaningfully participate in relationships that define us and enable us to grow.

Zizioulas contends that God only exists as Trinity, and without Trinity God cannot meaningfully exist. God only exists as a communion of three persons joined by the union of love. To put it another way, God's being as God only exists as a communion of the persons of the Trinity. Each person of the Trinity is transcended in the other, and hence there is infinite transcendence in the Trinitarian Godhead. A singular deity cannot exist meaningfully. This being, as communion – that is, the experience of the inner life of God the Trinity – is true of God's imminent life, as well as God's economic sending of the Son to invite all of us to participate in the intimacy of communion with Godself and others.

Like Rahner, Zizioulas insists that the Trinity relates to the people of the church, as they too only exist as persons who live in relation to other persons. Zizioulas asserts that:

> the being of God could be known only through personal relationships based on interpersonal relationships, which are also based on people being deeply vulnerable with

---

[231] Zizioulas, *The Eucharistic Communion and the World*, p. 20.

each other, which means we need deep trust in each other as the persons of the Trinity have among themselves in the one being. Being means life, and life means communion.[232]

God exists as Trinity, and He sent the Son into the world so that His followers can enter into an ongoing relationship with Him. This is crucial to a practical picture of God, as we live out relational life defined as togetherness. At a profound level, every follower of Jesus grows into Christ's likeness, as they are caused to transcend their present limitations to become more like Him. The divine Christ is always ahead of His people calling them to transcend themselves, but at the same time He empathises with them deeply because He knows human frailty personally. Zizioulas believes that as each of us partakes in the sacrament of Eucharist we are mysteriously and supernaturally partaking in deep intimacy with the God of the cross and that all of creation is potentially brought into communion with

---

Identity based on embracing diversity!

HOPE – Mission Organisation – UK

Together in words and action

'HOPE models what mission can look like, working with Christians of all ages, ethnicities, worship styles, genders and theological perspectives – together achieving much more than can be achieved apart. This lines up with Jesus' prayer that his followers would be "brought to complete unity" so that the world will know about God and his love for humanity (John 17:23).

'HOPE focuses on key mission moments – a rhythm of mission through the church calendar where churches can reach out into their communities.'

http://www.hopetogether.org.uk/Groups/256546/What_We_do.aspx.

For example: HOPE organised a multicultural festival a mission outreach – Inspire Magazine made this comment: 'Pentecost: Britain's multi-ethnic churches take to the streets.'

---

[232] Zizioulas, *Being as Communion*, p. 16.

the healing provided by the cross.[233] Indeed, all of life is summed up in the Eucharist for Zizioulas.[234] Through the Eucharist, the full transforming power of Christ is experienced through His sacrificial relationship with humanity, as it is worked out through His people, who sacrificially act as His hands, feet and words towards those impoverished for not knowing His real nature of sacrificial love.

However, Zizioulas does not leave communion with Christ alone. It is through the body of Christ, with each person as parts of Christ in the church, that each person is helped to transcend themselves, through the reciprocal relationships they have with other persons. The saying that 'iron sharpens iron' is far too weak to use in this context. However, it offers a useful metaphor for how every person in the body of Christ continues in a process of ecstatic transformation, becoming more like Christ as they grow, with His voice encouraging them to move forward. Only an infinite Christ can keep calling His people to further self-transcendence forevermore.

I have taken a few liberties in trying to bring out the full force of Zizioulas' Trinitarian communion theology. I have used some language and terminology not directly found in his writings. My aim has been to bring out some of the implications of his theology of communion so that its practical missional theological value can be demonstrated. The key value is that the missional church needs to provide more time for people to disciple each other, through the formation of deep friendships among peoples with whom we interact.

Jurgen Moltmann: The cross in the Trinity

Jurgen Moltmann takes Rahner's rule further than Rahner himself did. Moltmann's view of mutual interdependence between the persons of the Trinity is at the epicentre of his doctrine of God.[235] Moltmann considers, in similar vein to Zizioulas, that to be a person

---

233 Zizioulas, *The Eucharistic Communion and the World*, pp. 12-15.
234 Zizioulas, *The Eucharistic Communion and the World*, pp. 24-28.
235 Moltmann, *The Trinity and the Kingdom of God*, p. 19.

means to exist in relationship with others, so that we can know ourselves by comparison to others as separate persons to them. There are no persons without relationships. Relationships define who we are as persons in our own right. This is true of the Trinity. There is not a hierarchy of persons as such in the Trinity, but an egalitarian unity. The Father is not higher than the Son, neither is the Son more elevated than the Spirit. Each person of the Trinity shares in the life of the others, and each has a particular part in the process of salvation. Moreover, the persons in the Trinity are real persons. Person is not a function, neither is it simply a way of defining functions, as if functions were modes of being. The persons in the Godhead exist as persons defined by the other persons. The persons in the Trinity interrelate as real persons because They are united in Their one being as God.

The simplest way of describing this interrelational view of the Trinity is to speak of it as being socially founded. The Trinity, for Moltmann, is social in nature and therefore has deep interpersonal relationships between its persons. The divine persons also interact with human persons in the history of salvation. The history of salvation is all about the crucified God, who is actively incarnated in the lives of people. The climax of history for Moltmann is eschatological.[236] The God who has suffered for His world on the cross takes the world up into the eternal life of the Trinity. The people of God become part of God's eternal family in the fullest sense, when Jesus hands the redeemed cosmos into the Father's hands after the second coming.

This represents creation's complete renewal and full unification with the Father and His family. In Middle Eastern culture, the kingdom handed to the Father by the Son implied that the Father once again had a stable family to care for. However, this does not imply a hierarchical monarchy in the Godhead. Rather, fellowship with Father, Son and Holy Spirit is the driving narrative of the eternal kingdom. Where sacrificial love and fellowship exists there is no need to be concerned about God exercising abusive power

---

[236] Moltmann, *The Crucified God*, pp. 164-205.

over others, including over the Son or Spirit. If Son and Spirit are comfortable within the Father's reign as God themselves, then so can their creatures be comfortable. The Father becomes Father of all because the Son and Spirit have brought about unity and fellowship in the cosmos. Because the Trinity is defined as communion, God becomes all in all with no fears that He will ever transcend God's sacrificial nature of love which defines Godself, as God unchangeable. God will always exercise His love through service, not manipulation and overpowering domination.

Before Moltmann wrote his book *The Trinity and the Kingdom*, he produced his monograph, *The Crucified God*.[237] His theology of the cross follows the German reformer Luther's conviction that God is revealed in the suffering of the cross. The Christian God is not an unmoved deity. The God of the cross is passionate rather than passionless. This is what Moltmann terms 'theopathy': God joins in the suffering of the fallen creation in order to redeem and uplift creation into the resurrected life of Christ in the heavenlies.[238] This God of passion joins humankind in their suffering. God is in Christ suffering for the sins of humankind. Karkkainen comments on the significance of theopathy:

> The Son suffers the pain of being cut off from the life of the Father, and the Father suffers the pain of giving up the Son. By so doing, God 'also accepts and adopts it [suffering] in himself, making it part of his own eternal life.' Therefore, the cross is not an event only between God and humanity. For this theologian 'what happened on the cross was an event between God and God. It was a deep division in God himself, in so far as God abandoned God and contradicted himself, and at the same time a unity in God, in so far as God was at one with God and corresponded to himself.' Thus, the cross belongs to the

---

[237] Moltmann, *The Crucified God.*
[238] Moltmann, *The Crucified God*, p. 191-201.

inner life of God, not only occurring between God and estranged humanity.[239]

In other words, the cross of Christ has always been at the heart of the Trinity. The Trinity has always been theopathically defined. The cross of Christ is not an afterthought: if it had been, it would have meant that God's nature is not essentially defined by sacrificial love because an infinite God could not become omnibenevolent at some point. If God is infinite, then so is his sacrificial love. The cross defines the name of God; 'name' in biblical language means 'character'. God's character is ultimately hard to define.[240] However, I like to define it as being based on sacrificial love, as we see modelled in the cross of Christ.

The picture of God which most profoundly needs to be portrayed by the Christian community is the God of sacrifice and love. God sacrificially loves everyone to the point of the deepest sacrifice possible, as the Son is separated from the Father by bearing humanity's sin on the cross. God's love is self-sacrificial to the point that God gives up Godself in the person of the Son, when the Son cries out, 'My God, my God, why have you forsaken me?'[241] A practical theology of *missio Trinitatis* needs to have the theology of theopathy at its centre, as it is the foundation of the life of the church known as the body of Christ, the sacrificial Lord of creation. It needs to inform the church's participation with Christ, as Christ continues to identify with lost peoples through His people. Christ's people become a living picture of His sacrificial heart in action, as they sacrifice their own selves for others through selfless acts of love. This is at the heart of what God is like. This is the picture of God the Trinity on which we need to base our communities. Christ calls us to take up our crosses daily and to follow Him.[242]

---

[239] Karkkainen, *The Trinity*, p. 104.
[240] Brian Davies, *Philosophy of Religion: A Guide and Anthology*, Oxford: Oxford University Press (2000), p. 371.
[241] Mark 15:34.
[242] Luke 9:23-25.

Furthermore, Moltmann's belief that God is not a monarchy is very important to the Western socio-political environment. The Christian community needs to model kingdom-shaped society, in terms of egalitarian values lived out among its people. Living out these values will display to secular political culture a counter-narrative that is not defined by ego-driven individualism, but by shared values based on selfless love. It is also important to note that postmodern multicultural society is seeking to work more personalistically and relationally with the people it is there to represent and work with in the public square. We may argue that this, at least, is evidence that the Spirit is preparing the ground for a new counter-narrative based on God's selfless and sacrificial love – where service to others is the primary driver rather than self-service.

Moltmann contends that the monotheistic emphasis of classical theology led the early and later Western church towards a monarchical system of church governance in the form of bishops, who were known as patriarchs.

Identity based on spiritual formation into Christ's likeness!

St Andrew's Church, High Wycombe

'Our vision is to see our community transformed through a church that is alive with the joy of knowing and worshipping God, changed through living out His word, filled with His Spirit, living lives modeled on Jesus Christ and doing the works of the kingdom.

'More than a building, a name or a weekend gathering, St Andrew's is a community of people. We are living together the adventure for which God has created us, pursuing Christ and being changed by Him. At St Andrew's, community means connection and relationship, built on shared purpose and passion. It happens in weekly celebration services, in the smaller gatherings during the week, as we pray, serve and reach out to those around us, and in partnerships with other churches and organisations in this country and around the world.

'God doesn't want us to stay the same.'

http://sac-hw.org.uk/about-us

They had authority over the laity. Karkkainen suggests that 'notions of hierarchy, subordination and subjugation are foreign to [Moltmann's] social vision.'[243] Ultimately, this form of 'clerical monotheism' led to the papacy. By contrast, John 17 portrays the Christian community in very different terms:

> 'I do not pray for these only, but also for those who believe in me through their word, that they may all be one; even as thou, Father, art in me, and I in thee, that they also may be in us, so that the world may believe that thou hast sent me. The glory which thou hast given me I have given to them, that they may be one even as we are one.'[244]

In typical fashion, Moltmann applies his theology of *perichoresis*[245] to his vision of the Trinity, and to how the mutual interdependence true of the inner life is also to define the experiences of its community of disciples. Here we find no view of a hierarchical leadership system in the Christian community, where strong leaders seek to force their ideas on to a community of believers, such as some patriarchs in the early church did. In the Trinity-shaped missional community there is to be mutuality. Influence is won through deep friendships and relationships.

In true gospel of John terms, God's influence is at work in the mundane lives of believers who have strong meaningful relationships with each other. Joining in with the *missio Trinitatis* is intrinsic to the relational life of the egalitarian Christian community. This will mean that rather than it being manipulated by strong egocentric leaders who seek to impose their own versions of clerical monotheism, everyone in the community will serve God and others equally.

I am talking about the end of hierarchy. Where God's sacrificial love is to be found at work in a community, leaders will be servants

---

[243] Karkkainen, *The Trinity*, p. 114.

[244] John 17:20-22, RSV.

[245] *Perichoresis* means a harmonious dance where God and His people live in harmony together.

who equip others to serve as well. A circle of mutual service given in love is a definition of what a Trinity-shaped Christian community has as its modus operandi. Otherwise, mission can become the leader's pet project, and the leader becomes the community's driving force. This is a deep mystery which we still need help to grasp further, requiring that we learn to live out life in sacrificial love towards God and each other. Karkkainen captures Moltmann's conviction:

> On the one hand, creation and history are seen as part of a Trinitarian process that 'takes place in and with a God in whom there is no structure of domination, only a structure of equalitarian love.' On the other hand, 'the perichoretical relationships of love present in the Holy Trinity are the archetype of all relationships between different parts of the created reality including between human beings themselves.'[246]

In order for power not to be abused by hierarchical leadership structures, it is important for a missional community to be framed in a new way. Leadership will need to be exercised from the side rather than from the top. Leaders will need to learn to walk alongside people rather than imposing their power and ideas on them as requirements to be part of a church. They will need to actively listen to their people, seeking to help them speak what God is saying to them. This will hopefully help so-called apostles from going off on extraordinary flights of fancy, leading people to a new fantasy-ridden country where the leader's ego is stroked and reinforced by people following. The epistles of the apostle Paul indicate that Paul and his missionary helpers worked alongside the churches they planted, serving them rather than seeking to dominate them monarchically.[247]

---

[246] Karkkainen, *The Trinity*, p. 115.
[247] Moltmann offers a critique of monarchism, Moltmann, *The Trinity and the Kingdom of God*, pp.129-170. The apostle Paul spoke in humble not

The key concerns of Paul's leadership approach, as a model for servant leaders to follow, had to do with establishing people in their relationship with Christ and each other, so that the love of Christ could pour out into hearts by the Holy Spirit.[248] The Spirit of Christ needs to motivate His followers to become the voice of Christ that has every member engaged in servant leadership, equipping others to find Christ's voice for themselves and to discover His call on their lives, so that they can serve others in the community and lead them closer to the Christ of grace. Postmodern people do not go to our churches, according to the theologian John Drane, because they do not trust the leaders and authority structures that are portrayed by many of our churches.[249]

Peter Holmes and the social Trinity

Peter Holmes distinguishes himself not as a theologian, but rather as an applied psychologist and practical theologian to boot. He is the co-founder of Christ Church in Deal, Kent. He is also a member of the Chartered Management Institute, and of the Association of Therapeutic Communities. He has popularised his thinking about the Trinity in terms of the social Trinitarian vision of God.

The Trinity is a divine society that comes into applied pastoral psychology as 'the central issue in how faith' communities can 'better reflect the harmony and diversity of the Trinity.'[250] He addresses the key questions of practical and applied theology, as indicated by the title of his book, *Trinity in Human Community: Exploring Congregational Life in the Image of the Social Trinity.*

Holmes discusses the evolution of his practical psycho-social theology:

---

monarchical terms to the churches he wrote to, see for example, 1 Corinthians 2:1-5.

[248] Romans 5:5.

[249] John Drane, *Do Christians Know How to be Spiritual?*, chapter 2.

[250] Holmes, *Trinity in Human Community*, back cover.

Over the last few years I have been intrigued to realize the difference that a theology that understands God as social Trinity makes both to individuals and to faith communities. Instead of having an image of God as remote and individual (promoting a private one-to-one faith), it enables us to embrace a healthier image of a Trinity committed to promoting harmonic relationship. As Christians we begin to love a God who is never alone. This perception also creates a view of God that generates trust in relationships because He is already fully committed to permanent relationships. He already lives Trinity relationally. Consequently, since, however tarnished we may be, we are human beings made 'in his image'. We are intentionally created to thrive in the mutual giving and receiving of relationships. Like our Maker, we are all created for relationships. Such a view of God has the potential to transform us and all our 'relationships'.[251]

Following the theologian Colin Gunton, Holmes believes that the traditional static view of Western Christian theism (with the theme of an immutable and unknowable deity) has stunted the growth of Christian community life, making it difficult for a deeper kind of shared fellowship to exist among its people. He derives his thinking from a recognition that the heritage of Western theology has promoted a strong stand-alone individualism, where the oneness of God is emphasised over against the persons of the Trinity, in terms of their mutual interdependence and shared perichoretic love (or put another way, their mutually interdependent harmonious love dance). In his view, Father, Son and Spirit are joined in togetherness in continuous fellowship within the divine triadic relationship. Individualism has emphasised egotism as the driving narrative of Western egocentric society. Too many leaders in the church can succumb to this kind of egotism, which has found some of them inevitably seeking their

---

[251] Holmes, *Trinity in Human Community*, p. 5.

own selfish ends to the detriment of paying due respect for all with whom they are co-equals in the body of Christ.

The early church's view (fourth, fifth and sixth centuries AD) of the one God came before the three persons who were defined in the language of the Trinity, first of all at the council of Nicaea (323 AD). In other words, the unchangeable nature of the one God overshadowed the diversity of the persons in the triadic union. If God was simply to be thought of as transcendent and impersonal, then there was no possibility of a Christian community experiencing communion and community with Him.

The Trinity, in the view of St Augustine (sixth century AD), and later also of Aquinas (thirteenth century AD), could not countenance a mutual view of a God who could be changed, based on the whim and fancy of those He had created. In other words, God's mind could not be changed by human petitions, because a perfect God knows everything and does not need to change His mind based on mutable human prayer. This view went forward into Reformation Protestantism and later Evangelical views of God in the West. It considers the main task of mission to be to bring people to the point where they accept Christ, and then to consider the job done. In my view, this approach misses the gospel narratives where the disciples were shaped by following Jesus. Of course, things are changing, and discipleship formation is now a growing practice in some Christian contexts.

The lack of a social Trinitarian vision of God seems to hamper clear practical theological reflection for people of faith, because they do not shape their identities on a God of intimate inter-relations, which a social Trinitarian view of the Trinity provides. God is distanced. It is important that Christians engage in theological reflection, in order to understand and practically apply ideas about God to the way their communities form their identities, based on their vision of God. After all, theology is the study of God and what He is like. Hence we need to reflect theologically.[252] Holmes'

---

[252] Judith Thompson, *Theological Reflection*, London: SCM Press (2012), pp. 1-34.

theological reflections follow a similar vein to Barth's and Rahner's, where God enters into history through the Word and through Christ, meaning that human life is now part of God's life in some mysterious sense.

Holmes follows Zizioulas, where the persons of the Trinity are defined as real persons only by Their inter-relationships. Moreover, according to Holmes, the people of the missional community are defined by their inter-relations with the Spirit of Christ. The Spirit of Christ is recognised to be an intimate presence in disciples' hearts, enabling His followers to be joined in communion with the dynamic living God. Moreover, relationships between Christians are meant to help people form deeper communion with each other and with God.[253] Christ leads His disciples so that they continue to transcend themselves, becoming more like Him and engaging with His Spirit in His continuing mission to the world. A community that operates in this way will inevitably frame a compelling picture of the God who joins in with the lives of people in the world. Holmes agrees with Moltmann that the God of social Trinity is conceived to be deeply engaged in the joys and sorrows of people's ordinary lives in the processes of contemporary society.

Conclusions

These connections in the thinking of our Trinitarian theologians are a good starting point to round up and conclude this chapter to provide a pastiche of my theology of MT. The social Trinity is an evolution of theological thought that has grown to maturity, particularly in the light of Holmes' postmodern psycho-sociology. It is his work particularly that practically integrates the thinking of other theologians like the four I have discussed into practical pastoral psychology. Hence my pastiche is drawn together in the light of his applied psycho-social theology of the social Trinity. People cannot be understood unless we understand them in the

---

253 Simon Reed, *Creating Community: Ancient Ways for Modern Churches,* Abingdon: The Bible Reading Fellowship (2013), pp. 34-39.

context of the relationships they have with each other and God in practical theology. In order for multicultural missional communities to function, they need to be based on a social theology of the Trinity that is founded on a reasonable psycho-social platform. Holmes' work does this for us. In the light of his work I have constructed the theology of the next chapter using a contextualisation of the social Trinity which can relate to men, women and their offspring.

Holmes' approach to the social Trinity is based on the inner work of the Holy Spirit, as well as on the healthy psycho-social functioning of a Trinity-shaped family or community. Human relationships need to be infused with the Spirit of the Trinity in order to help them see themselves reflected in others who are also being transformed into Christ's likeness as they live together with others in the body of Christ. By interacting with persons made in the *imago Christi*, they see themselves reflected in the same way as persons who exist in relationships with other Christian persons. According to the apostle Paul, no one is sufficient unto themselves in the body of Christ.[254] Rather, we all need to serve each other and to receive what Christ is offering to each of us through other people. These relationships make up the organic functions we need to survive through His body of peoples that sustains our spiritual lives. No one person will ever be completely like Christ, because Christ exists through His body, where each organ of the body fulfils a vital service to be received by other parts of the body.

The MT is at work through our missional communities. The people of these communities are directly involved in portraying God's love for His creation in ongoing human history, in their local communities. Communities that shape their identities in the likeness of Christ will incarnate a picture of Christ to those they seek to disciple. Scripture and the community help us to weigh the revelation of the Holy Spirit, and what it means to apply that in our lives. Christian lives lived out in multicultural society, and in our Christian communities, need to be tested by the benchmark of

---

[254] Ephesians 2:8-10.

Scripture, reason, experience and tradition. We need to discern the *missio Trinitatis* based on the triangulation of discerning God's will through Scripture, personal community experiences and evidences of the Trinity's work ahead of the church in our social contexts.

Chapter 8
A picture of the Trinity suited to multicultural society

What I write in this chapter may be completely countercultural to your understanding of the Trinity, in which the Father, Son and Spirit all attract the use of the masculine pronoun and do not allow for the use of the feminine pronoun. In what I share in this chapter, I construct another interpretation of the Trinity as Father, Mother (Spirit), Son and Daughter (offspring). The portrayal of the masculine, feminine and child aspects in God's nature offers a liberation narrative that is much needed in a world where women are too often discriminated against, and where vulnerable children are too often abused in a variety of ways by adults who exercise abusive power over them, or of course by their peers. My picture of the Trinity is one where Godself is non-discriminating, and our multicultural society in the West witnesses much discrimination, as indeed is true of peoples in all world nations. As I mentioned in the introduction to chapter 7, I use family analogically when I speak of Trinity as family. This analogy does not take away from God's omnipotence, omniscience, omnibenevolence, omnipresence and infinite underived eternal being as God. Human families are a different category from the Trinity family. It is by undeserved grace that human families are made part of the eternal Trinity's family by adoption in Christ.

In this chapter I hope to provide analogies of how my practical missional theology works in practice in the reflections that follow. When my son and daughter were teenagers, they were intrigued and confused by the idea of the Trinity. How could God be one and yet three persons? As parents, Jenny and I wondered whether the idea of Trinity was of any relevance to the emerging generations, which sociologists call Generations Y and Z. In a youth church that Jenny and I started, which both churched and unchurched young people attended, we soon discovered they also found it hard to make three into one or one into three. The mathematics of the Trinity made no sense to them.

When we started to speak of Godself as a united family made up of Father, Son and Mother (Spirit), they took hold of this and found it much more helpful. They could appreciate that they were part of God's family which united them by His love. It also became significant to them that they were God's sons and daughters. Moreover, it helped to forge their identities as children of Father and Mother God's eternal family. An eternal family had the appeal of being secure, and of lasting endurance, compared to some of their home backgrounds where parents had split up or divorced. I found myself wondering whether the picture of the Trinity as a family would prove appealing to other young people.

A very interesting insight from research literature is that Generations Y and Z hold families much more dearly than perhaps their forebears did (those of Generation X). What these two emerging generations seem to be looking for are stable role models among peers and trusted adults to help shape their lives. Moreover, a family does not have to be a young person's biological parents. A few of my colleagues have suggested to me that young adults, especially, respond well to trusted spiritual role models who are what might be called 'spiritual fathers and mothers'.

The picture of Trinity as Father, Mother and offspring is a wonderful idea that I believe we need to further construct and use in order to shape how our Christian communities can provide spiritual fathers, mothers, brothers and sisters to these generations as a picture of God portrayed through the body of Christ. Such persons can hopefully walk alongside late teens or young adults to disciple them to become lifelong followers of Christ. These spiritual parents, or siblings, will need to act as intelligent mirrors, reflecting back ideas and providing a means to increase self-awareness for less-experienced faith-seekers.

Coming back to the youth community we began with, it is worth observing that these young people found helpful the idea that they had a divine Father, Mother and elder Brother/Sister with whom they could share their challenges. They also recognised that their youth group was a community of brothers and sisters, on whom they could rely for support in the context of God's family. Trinity family became a useful metaphor for identifying the family we all belonged to, and the community helped them to remain firm in their Christian journey as they lived out their lives at school and with their peers. The group acted on the basis of a shared communion, where the youth could more intimately connect with Godself as a selfless, caring parent.

> **Identity based on Christ-like selfless service towards others!**
>
> Grace Family Church – Liverpool
>
> 'Our Vision: "Building a relevant 21st Century Church that is passionate about God and reaches into people's lives with His love, transforming and empowering them to become leaders in their generation, impacting and changing the world."'
>
> One of their core values is 'Service: Jesus selflessly served, assisted, guided and taught others throughout His entire ministry. As brothers and sisters in Christ we endeavour to serve each other.'
>
> http://www.gracefamilychurch.co.uk/about-us/our-vision
>
> http://www.gracefamilychurch.co.uk/about-us/our-values

It also helped the group members to define their community as a communion, where each person could more transparently share their struggles with one another. Obviously, trust was important to build, and took time to foster. We followed the simple rule that the young people could share anything, however challenging, as part of the group. We encouraged them to view God as their heavenly parent who would not leave them to struggle through their personal issues alone; neither would their peers, as part of His family. We noticed that they became more confident in their prayer lives, and in the ways they sought to bring God into the things they were doing.

The youth church I am referring to only lasted as long as these young people lived at home with their parents. When they moved on to university, or to work, they were encouraged to form friendships that would help to sustain their faith in their new contexts. Many succeeded in doing this. The kinds of friendships they formed could be described as soul friendships, where they identified friends who deeply shared their values.

It was good that we were able to be one of the influences that prepared these young people for the next steps in their lives. Moreover, they organised themselves outside the youth church context and would meet up to do other things together.

Some of these young people have remained strong Christians as they have journeyed into adult life. Some came from Christian families; others did not. What struck Jenny and me was the importance of providing strong role models, upon which they could build their own identities. Moreover, these young people became far better at relating to their siblings and their parents at home, where some had struggled before. They obtained a new view of the importance of family life, because God was their family, and this in turn focused their attention on its importance and value.

Contextual analogy of the Trinity to the human family

Having made these comments, it is important to remind ourselves of the huge strains that postmodern and migrant families face in the West. The potential breakdown of as many as one in every two marriages has huge repercussions for everyone, including young adults, as they contemplate who their future life partners might be. Of course, it is increasingly trendy for young Western adults in their twenties to share life with their peers in what we have already identified as new tribes.[255] It is also true that marriage is not the only option available for young adults, as they live with partners of the same or opposite sex. Children often grow up with a father or mother other than their birth father or mother. Others grow up in single-parent families or same-sex families. These diverse experiences help to inform their opinions of whether marriage is worthwhile or not.

In the light of this rather fragmented situation, talking of God as a family made up of Father, Mother and Child, or of a Christian community as a family, would seem to need some clear definition. The inclusion of the feminine aspect in God is a strong theme among feminist theologians.[256] Motherhood is an important part of how offspring are shaped in the human community.[257] Moreover, the broader view of the masculine and feminine in what it means to be human has to be part of the narrative of Father, Mother and Child existing in the Trinity. Many young people entering into adult life do so without the belief that their fathers or mothers are worthy of respect, because of parental neglect, abuse, selfishness or divorce and separation. For example, how can a young woman who was raised by her mother really understand what it feels like to have a father, if her father was absent during her formative years. In same-sex families, there is the increased complexity of the lack of a male or female role model.

I write none of this to be judgemental, but rather to be realistic. The missional church of the twenty-first century needs to contemplate this new situation, especially given that many who come to faith now and in the future will increasingly be involved in same-sex partnerships – and many will have offspring who have been adopted or surrogated.

---

[255] Ethan Watters, *Urban Tribes: Are Friends the New Family?* London: Bloomsbury (2004), pp. 1-14.

[256] Mary McClintock Fulkerson and Sheila Briggs, *The Oxford Handbook of Feminist Theology,* Oxford: Oxford University Press (2013), pp. 372-374; 371-381.

[257] Laurie Cassidy and Maureen H. O'Connell (eds.), *She Who Imagines: Feminist Theological Aesthetics,* Collegeville: Liturgical Press (2012), pp. 53-69.

Much of what I write below about the Trinity shape of family life may take on a new contextual description in the light of this trend, including how missional churches seek to integrate such families into their Christian communities. How can a young adult who was abused, mentally, physically or sexually, by their father or mother (man or woman), come to trust Father God or

Mother Spirit? If our psyches are at times so undermined in terms of trusting our own parents, how can the picture of God as Father, Mother (Spirit) and Son be attractive, or useful, to some of the members of Generations Y and Z? How will same-sex families be integrated into a Trinitarian Christian family? New emerging versions of what society defines as a family are changing rapidly.

Missional Christian communities are already asking how they can helpfully respond to these new types of families. The challenge some are facing is that faith-seekers with same-sex partners who have children want to raise their families as Christians. Of course, Christian communities have a variety of opinions on how to respond to these emergent challenges. What we all need to ask ourselves is, 'What is Godself, as Trinity family, saying to us about how we should participate in life together, with those who deeply love God, who make up these newly defined kinds of families?'

These are not easy questions to ask. And it is vital to note that just as those born in the West have these fragmented experiences of family life, it is the same for young people who belong to other ethnicities and cultures who are now living in the West. I know of many families in Christian ethnic communities living in the UK that involve separated or divorced parents, or where children have been abused or neglected by their caregivers. None of this is to cast blame anywhere; it is simply important to realise that all Christian ethnic churches, including white ethnic churches, have families who have had, or are going through, deeply troubling experiences.

So is it at all useful, or appropriate, to speak of the Trinity as a family to which we can belong? I have already shared my basic conviction above, where I suggested that Generations Y and Z,[258] and the third culture young people of migrant Christian families,[259] seem to be joining together in their own tribe-like communities, seeking to be supportive families to their peers. The term third culture is defined with the recognition that migrant families entering into a new culture raise their children to take on their originating culture's values. However, their children also need to be able to take on elements of the new culture among which they live. They are caught between both cultures. Hence they form their own kind of third culture, which is an amalgam of their parents' culture and the new one, but not the same as either, making it a third adapted new culture. It seems that the Spirit may be prophetically calling the church to follow Her work as She seeks to nourish and nurture these young adults, who want to find a real home within which to base their relationships. Surely the Trinity family is relevant as a bridge to help men, women and children find their home in the Father, Son and Mother's (Spirit's) home.

Moreover, research among those who might be called Generation Y highlights that these young adults highly value family life, even if their families are their tribe-like communities during their young adult years. There is evidence that young adults who are becoming Christians from Generation Y, particularly, are looking for trustworthy role models who can act as spiritual fathers

---

[258] *The Telegraph*, 'Gen Z, Gen Y, baby boomers – a guide to the generations'. Available at http://www.telegraph.co.uk/news/features/11002767/Gen-Z-Gen-Y-baby-boomers-a-guide-to-the-generations.html (accessed 9th October 2015).
[259] Andrew R. Hardy, and Dan Yarnell, *Forming Multicultural Partnerships: Church Planting in a Divided Society*, Watford: Instant Apostle (2015), pp.114-140.

and mothers for them, as I have already noted. I have noticed this phenomenon among young adults who train on ForMission College's[260] placement-based ministry courses. I believe this notion will become as widespread among the emergent members of Generation Z. If this is the case, the idea of Trinity family, made up of the loving sacrificial Father, Son and Mother (Holy Spirit), will provide Christian missional communities with an appropriate picture of God as a family and a home that welcomes all of these new, emerging subcultural expressions.

Providing a meaningful account of how humanity became broken

In order to help Generations Y and Z and third culture young adults to understand how the world of imperfect broken families came about, we need to provide a social and psychological understanding of what fractures human family life. It would seem like a valuable starting point to consider the creation narratives in Genesis chapters 1, 2 and 3 from a psycho-social point of view. In these chapters, humankind and God are set in what may be defined in terms of a relational view of human interactions. I believe that this same God still desires to walk alongside us, as He did in the primordial Garden of Eden.[261]

Humankind is asserted to have been made in *Elohim*'s (Hebrew word for God, meaning Gods – plural) social image, according to the writer of Genesis.[262] According to Genesis, Elohim made families as the fundamental building blocks of society.[263] The view of the Ancient Near East, found as it is in the story of Elohim calling on the heavenly sons of God (angels) to participate with Him in the

---

[260] ForMission College. Details available at http://formission.org.uk/ (accessed 9th October 2015).

[261] Genesis 3:8. Also see Day's study of Genesis chapters 1–3, John Day, *From Creation to Babel: Studies in Genesis 1–11*, London: Bloomsbury T & T Clark (2015), pp. 1-50.

[262] Genesis 1:26-27.

[263] Genesis 2:24-25.

creation of humankind,[264] eventually led to John's description of a kind of divine triad existing between the Father, Son and Spirit as the creators of humans. Father, Son and Spirit are portrayed in John's gospel as a unified family.[265] The early church thought that God was best described as three persons united in one being. It is also not hard to imagine how the early church fathers noticed that Elohim, as a plural form, calling out, 'Let us make humankind in our image,' implies the Trinity.

I take further imaginative licence by noting that in Genesis 1:2, the Spirit, from the Hebrew noun *Ruach*, was hovering over the amniotic birthing waters of chaos, expectantly looking for creation to come forth from Her womb. I call *Ruach* (Spirit) 'Her' because the word is in the feminine in the Hebrew, as well as in Semite thought.

This is why I prefer to speak of the Holy Spirit as the feminine aspect of God. It provides a more egalitarian picture of humankind as man, woman and offspring which together are said to make up the *imago Dei* in Genesis 1:26-27. We cannot speak too literally here, of course. But I find it useful to recognise that humankind was made in God's image, male and female. The Old and New Testaments use masculine and feminine language to describe God.[266]

Moreover, we may picture the conception of the Son of God as Mother Spirit implanting the Father's Son in Mary's womb. The Spirit was pregnant with the child of God. By the miracle of this divine union with Mary's ovum the God-man came into being.

The idea of God's Word becoming incarnate can also, to some extent, be derived from developments of Plato's thought in the first century. In Plato's thought, the Word (Greek *Logos* in John's gospel) was the design agent behind the structured ordered world of

---

[264] Genesis 1:26-27. Day, *From Creation to Babel,* p. 12.

[265] John 5:19, 20.

[266] The Hebrew word for Spirit is *Ruach* which is in the feminine tense. Genesis 1:1, 2, 26, 27; 2:7; Numbers 11:12; Deuteronomy 32:11, 18; Hosea 11:1-4; Isaiah 42:14; Isaiah 45:10; Isaiah 49:15; Isaiah 66:13; Proverbs 1:20; Matthew 11:19; 23:37; John 3:5-6.

creation, which John says the Son of God was involved in creating as part of Godself.[267]

It seems that John saw the connection of the Word (*Logos*) to the idea found in Proverbs regarding the work of Lady Wisdom, as she stood at Yahweh's side during the creation of the world. Mother Spirit and Father Yahweh brought forth creation through Their eternal Son, who was the agent of Creation according to John's gospel (See John 1:1-8). The Son, as Word of God, is the founder of the birth of the peoples and structures that support them in this created world. These peoples are His brothers and sisters whom Father and Mother (Spirit) brought forth through Their eternal offspring. Lady Wisdom in Proverbs 8 is clearly taken from the idea of God's feminine aspect, which was involved in the birth of the cosmos. It is important to consider Lady Wisdom's actions, personified as they are in Proverbs 8:

> The LORD brought me [Lady Wisdom] forth as the first of
> his works,
> before his deeds of old;
> I was formed long ages ago,
> at the very beginning, when the world came to be.
> When there were no watery depths, I was given birth,
> when there were no springs overflowing with water;
> before the mountains were settled in place,
> before the hills, I was given birth,
> before he made the world or its fields
> or any of the dust of the earth.
> I was there when he set the heavens in place,
> when he marked out the horizon on the face of the deep,
> when he established the clouds above
> and fixed securely the fountains of the deep,
> when he gave the sea its boundary
> so that the waters would not overstep his command,
> and when he marked out the foundations of the earth.

---

[267] 'In the beginning was the λόγος ... (John 1:1)'. Available at
http://www.bible-researcher.com/logos.html (accessed 9th October 2015).

Then I was constantly at his side.
I was filled with delight day after day,
rejoicing always in his presence,
rejoicing in his whole world
and delighting in the human race.[268]

Lady Wisdom is portrayed by the writer of Proverbs chapters 1–8 as she addresses her sons, giving them counsel to help them move into adult life.[269] These children were to be thought of as the young people of Israel, who were being nurtured to heed the counsel of God's deep mysterious wisdom. The concept of the feminine aspect of God, as the conveyor of God's deep wisdom, coming in Hebrew wisdom literature to personification was of great importance for the developments that later took place in John's gospel. The divine Word becoming a human being translates God into human relational language.

The general concept of the design agency of the Word (*Logos*), for Middle-Platonism, was that of the intelligent design agent behind the material creation. Of course, this is a very simplified account. This broadly could be thought of as resonating with the idea of Lady Wisdom, as the one who was at Yahweh's side during creation, intelligently forming the world as it was fashioned by God.

Some theologians have recognised the importance of recognising John's Word theology and its probable reliance on the wisdom traditions as we see it expressed in passages like Proverbs 8. Of course, in John's gospel Jesus Christ is no less than the divine eternal Son of the Father (Yahweh – see John 1:14, 18). He came out of the passionate, throbbing heart of the Father.[270] He translates God's heart into a human being who lived by the passion coming from His Father's heart. Christ is male because the birth of a Daughter of God would not have been acceptable in Greco–Roman society to represent the reign of God.

---

[268] Proverbs 8:22-31 (NIVUK).
[269] Proverbs 1:20; 2:1; 3:1; 4:1; 5:1; 6:1; 7:1; 8:1.
[270] John 1:18.

The Word of wisdom was God, in other words, who became flesh, having come out of the communion the Son shared with the Father and Mother's heart (John 1:1). It was this divine Word that intelligently designed the world we all inhabit, according to John 1:1-18.

The Spirit, as Mother of creation, can also be recognised as another divine person, the Spirit in John's gospel. Yet John uses the masculine pronoun to identify the Spirit.[271] This use of the masculine to describe Father, Son and Spirit in John must not be used to argue that God only welcomes the masculine aspect in humanity. Rather, John probably used it because, in the context of Greco–Roman and Jewish society, family was identified with the *pater familias* (the father figure as the accepted representation of the whole family, including women and children). Feminist theologians have done much by their insistence on the feminine aspect in God to address the millennia-old patriarchialism of male-dominated cultures.[272] In the Old Testament, the feminine is used to describe God and His Spirit in numerous instances. We also find Christ using feminine language as He weeps over Jerusalem, declaring His desire to protect them as a mother hen protects her chicks under her wings.[273]

John's idea of the Son of God being eternal and co-equal with God was shocking to the extreme in terms of classical Jewish thought of the first century. How could God become flesh? The idea that wisdom personified, in passages like Proverbs 8, took on human form was probably less worrying to ancient Jews, because Hebrew poetry often used real children, born to earthly parents, to represent divine actions in human society.[274] These children, in the cases of Isaiah and Hosea, for example,[275] were either male or female. So the Word could be said to have been a metaphor John

---

[271] John 16:13.
[272] McClintock Fulkerson, Briggs, *The Oxford Handbook of Feminist Theology*, p. 73.
[273] Matthew 23:37.
[274] Isaiah 7:10-17.
[275] Hosea 1:1-11.

used to express the idea that the Son of God was at God's side at creation, without implying that God was to be considered as male only.

This latter view has been emphasised by some feminist scholars, and those who share their views about the feminine in God, or the Spirit of God.[276] However, it seems very hard to push the argument to the extent that they and others do, when the plain reading of John 1:1 expresses the divinity of the Son of God, especially when it is compared to John 8:58 where Jesus claims that He is 'I am', which directly relates to the passage in Exodus 3 when Yahweh speaks as the 'I am' through His angel. Some early Jews who became devotees to Jesus the Messiah almost certainly worshipped Him as Yahweh. This can be identified by the early use of the Aramaic word *Maranatha*, literally meaning, 'Lord, come'. It was addressed directly to Jesus, using the Aramaic equivalent of 'Yahweh' to address Jesus, when early Christian Jews worshipped God probably within days of the Lord's resurrection and Pentecost.[277]

Toward the latter part of the first century AD, when John was writing his gospel, it was far easier to bring out what had been latent in the first generation of Christian belief about the divinity of Christ. As thoughtful Christians of the fourth, fifth and sixth centuries continued to contemplate John's views about Father, Son and Spirit, the creeds were formulated. These creeds helped to formulate the church's confession of the doctrine of the Trinity, which was officially sanctioned with the Nicene Creed in the early part of the fourth century AD. It was further ratified at the council of Constantinople (AD 381).

The framers of the early creeds, in the fourth century, needed to define how there could be more than one divine person in the one God. Bishop Arius contended during the fourth century that Christ was not divine but a created being. The Nicene Creed was formulated to counter Arius' belief. After all, John's gospel had

---

[276] McClintock Fulkerson, Briggs, *The Oxford Handbook of Feminist Theology*, pp. 372-373.; Veli-Matti Karkkainen, (2002), *Pneumatology*, pp. 165-166, 167.
[277] Hurtado, *Lord Jesus Christ*, pp. 21, 110, 111, 136, 141, 143, 172-175, 198.

taken the theological step of recognising that the master he had known so well was none other than God's Divine Son, although I believe that Christ was worshipped as divine Son of God in the time of the writing of Mark's gospel as well (see Mark 1:1).

As we have discussed, Eastern Orthodox theologians developed this insight further, by formulating the concept of the social Trinity,[278] which was first articulated by the Cappadocian Fathers during the period in which the doctrine of the Trinity came to expression in the creeds. We might add that Father, Son and Spirit were the three persons in the one being of Genesis' Elohim, who were the 'us' who made humankind in Elohim's 'image and 'likeness'.[279] When Elohim called on the angels saying, 'Let us make humankind in our image', He was celebrating the image of God which defined the other heavenly beings He had made. In other words, it is as though Elohim were declaring, 'Will it not be wonderful to create humankind so they too can enjoy the life we all share in our relational communion together!' Perhaps I take too much imaginative licence here!

It is important to make a connection between the previous chapter and this one. According to theologians like John Zizioulas, there is no being without relationship.[280] In his view, much like the theologian Jurgen Moltmann, Trinity can be thought of as a relational interaction between Father, Son and Spirit. Taken in these terms, God may be said to be, at heart, a set of deeply inter-connected relationships which occur between the divine persons. This strongly implies that He also reveals himself naturally to humankind as a divine family. The Elohim of Genesis created humankind in His relational image. Relationship is found in every book of the Bible and is integral to human design and God's nature. It is intrinsic and extrinsic to the theology of the Bible.

---

[278] Holmes, *Trinity in Human Community*, pp. 6, 15, 21, 28, 36, 38, 41, 46, 49, 65, 75, 90, 110, 144, 146, 169, 170, 175, 181.

[279] Holmes, *Trinity in Human Community*, p. 49.

[280] Zizioulas, *Being as Communion*, pp. 15-65.

This would make the image of God in humankind most readily recognised by our tendency to define our own lives by the relationships we have with each other, in families and friendships particularly. Human families act as micro-communities that shape their children through their deep relationships to become functional, empathic persons in their own right. The Christian community, as the macro-community of Father, Son and Mother (Spirit), also has the role of forming its participants through relationships between Godself and Their earthly offspring.

At the heart of the Christian community is God the family, which shares in the Trinity family's life cycle. It is the role of the nurturing Mother Spirit to bring to life healing, wholeness, forgiveness, care, support, mercy and sacrificial love in Christian communities. Jesus declared at a Jewish feast that pure holy waters would metaphorically gush from Christian bellies after Pentecost, coming from the divine wellspring of the Spirit of God.[281]

The Mother Spirit nurtures the family and helps it thrive. This might seem to make the image of God in humankind only attainable by people who participate in genuine Christian life. The small units of this Trinity likeness are portrayed in family life, which microcosmically is made up of parents and offspring, and macrocosmically in mutuality and interdependence with brothers and sisters in Trinity's broader Christian family. This narrative of people being formed as they live in sacrificially loving relationships together, and within Trinity family, forms a compelling picture, in my view, of the Father, Son and Mother who may be viewed as spiritually present at the centre of each Christian family.

The picture of God in families where partners become one

According to Genesis 2:24-25, the reason why a man and a woman were to leave their fathers and mothers was so that they could become 'one flesh' in a mutually cohesive relationship, which was

---

[281] John 7:38-39.

to model itself on the union they shared together with Elohim. The idea behind the Hebrew word for 'unite' is descriptive of the cleaving of marriage partners who are welded together in a deep, trusting relationship. The word suggests an inseparable bond at a far deeper level than sexual union. It means inseparable unitedness. This union is of heart, spirit, body and life experiences. Paul uses the unification imagery of marriage as a deep symbol to describe Christ's love for the church.[282]

The Greek term *Ekklesia* (an intentional community gathering) meant far more than a club in ancient society. It was conceived of as a polis, or an official gathering of people in Greco–Roman society who lived closely in a community, in order to make important decisions for the community. In Christian terms this missional polis was a community in which all people would need to share equally – male, female, slave and free.[283] According to Paul, no higher or lower regard was to be exercised or expressed towards any person in this polis.[284] Jesus, of course, says the same when He pictures all disciples as servants of one another in His kingdom community, on earth as well as in heaven.[285] The foundation of God's community could be thought of as a marriage-like welding together of all brothers and sisters as parts of one body, where each member was reliant on the others, and no one member had a monopoly over others.[286]

The other way of talking of a self-sustaining, caring body can be as our participation together in Father, Son and Spirit's Trinitarian family, as a lived out life with them in our Christian communities.

In terms of what marriage implies for the Christian couple, there is a very special sense in which joining together implies sharing naked inner life together, to the core of their souls, based on their inseparable union. The concept of penetration is at one level a literal sexual act, as expressed in Genesis 2:24-25. However, mutual

---

[282] Ephesians 5:25.
[283] Galatians 3:28.
[284] Galatians 3:28.
[285] Matthew 23:11.
[286] 1 Corinthians 12:12-31.

interpenetration is a metaphorical description of the Trinity's relationship, suggested to be Father, Son and Spirit living Their life in oneness by being 'in' one another together in mystical union. This is language of deep, interpenetrative intimacy and love which togetherness brings.

It seems that the wedded union of married life can be seen as a mirroring of the intimacy of the divine life. Humankind is made in Trinity's image. *Perichoresis* is the Greek word that the church fathers used to describe this divine inter-relational mutuality of love. It has been well described as mutual interpenetration of each member of the Godhead, as the deep, united life of love between the persons of God. It is this united shared being as 'one flesh' which makes the divine persons the one God of monotheism.

What this implies to me is that the oneness that earthly families need to explore is a means that God established between man and woman, as partakers in His image, and the *perichoresis* in which He wants them to participate with Father, Mother (Spirit)[287] and Son (Child or Daughter). Humankind, made in Trinity's image as human families, has at least three components – a father, a mother and offspring (in traditional terms, at the very least). This is what it means to be human.

Jesus Christ, the male human child, could just as easily have been a female had He been born in a culture based on matriarchal norms and values. Jesus the male could have been female if we use insights from contextual theology which help us to understand that God incarnated in the Jewish culture through the Son because it was a patriarchal culture, as was most of the Greco–Roman world at that time. Young women and young men in our families can relate to the Trinity family because it is inclusive of the masculine and feminine, as humankind was made in the *imago Trinitatis*. Moreover, even those who mistrust their parents can still relate to the masculine and feminine, which is part of the architecture of my view of what it

---

[287] Leonardo Boff helps us to understand how the feminine is in the Spirit as it is in humanity: Leonardo Boff, *Cry of the Earth, Cry of the Poor*, Maryknoll: Orbis Books (1997), pp. 169-171.

means to be partakers of *imago Trinitatis*. It is important to remember, however, that the use of the feminine pronoun to describe God can be deeply offensive in many cultural contexts. My argument is that we need to recognise that the writer of Genesis clearly locates the feminine in God.

Our families need to base their picture of family love, trust and life lived out intimately in togetherness on actual participation with the Spirit in terms of the eternal intimacy of the united divine three. Our Christian community families need to develop members who can intimately participate in God's loving family of fathers, mothers, sisters and brothers. Trinity-shaped Christian communities need to be nurtured by the Spirit of God to share ever more deeply in love-based relationships showing deep respect to one another.

In a sense, the family is its own kind of expression of the Trinity's *perichoresis*, which I believe is fundamentally hard-wired into human identity. This is why we can never assume that humankind, made in Trinity's relational image, can do without the living picture of Trinity's love and togetherness at the heart of its missional communities. We can find case studies of this divine intimacy in the synoptic gospels, and even more directly in John's gospel, which give us an insight into the Father and Son's intimate shared life and mission to make disciples who are children of God's family.[288]

Ultimately the Christian missional community continues to reach out to welcome new participants, so that people may reach wholeness as partakers in the Trinity's eternal family as far as the finite can participate in the infinite divine life. I suggest the Trinity shapes Christian families and communities to become authentic, functional families, where love abounds to cover a multitude of sins.[289] The Spirit provides the eternal presence of God's love in the hearts of persons who belong to God's family.

The diagram on the following page shows the triangulation of Mother (Spirit), Father and Child in the Trinity. It also represents

---

[288] John 1:12; 21:5; Matthew 18:1-4; Matthew 19:13; Luke 18:15-17.
[289] 1 Peter 4:8.

what humankind was designed to be like, in order to shape its offspring as part of a Trinity-like society. All of human society was fundamentally designed to be Trinitarian in nature, in my view. Hence the picture of God displayed by our Christian communities needs to frame the new identity that secular society needs to discover and base its structures upon.

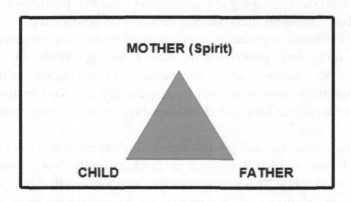

Humans, as the image-bearers of the Trinity's family, were made to exist in intimate, participative relationships, defined by togetherness, peaceful co-existence and loving service. Fallen society keeps on running from the image of intimacy which men, women and children are called to share with God, because we fear becoming naked and vulnerable, as it will cause us to lose hold of our egotistic control mechanisms, which are part of our IWMs.[290]

According to Genesis 2:24-25, intimacy is based on naked vulnerability. Nakedness includes the need for trust and transparency in the Christian family, which will expose each of us as the derelict and helpless creature we are, if left to ourselves. Yet man and woman were originally made naked, symbolising the deep, transparent nakedness which was designed into humanity made in *imago Trinitatis*. Human society needs to be healed by the creative nurturing Mother (Spirit). Each of us needs to allow

---

[290] Internal working models. See 'Attachment to the family of God' in chapter 3.

ourselves, our families and our loved ones to be healed by vulnerably opening our inner beings to the Father, with whom we all can be honest and without fear of abuse, manipulation or rejection. Our Christian communities need to become safe places where we can be transparent with each other without the risk of abuse.

This is why the Trinity narrative is so vital to portray as the picture of God to Generations Y and Z, because their attempts to find belonging in small tribe-like gatherings of trusted peers is actually a deep organic cry from their delicate and fractured inner child. They need to find their true reality and identity in Trinity-shaped, family-like communities. By finding their real identities in these communities, they will be able to form their families, and broader society, to rediscover the *imago Trinitatis* which is the foundation for all human families and communities.

The missing ingredient is the need to intimately connect with Father, Mother (Spirit) and Son, who desire to be present, dwelling in their midst, so that They can heal fractured human hearts. Christ the one true Son of God offers each of us the opportunity to participate with His Spirit in the formation of our hearts and lives into His likeness, as we model our identities upon the life of Christ, the new Adam.[291] This is why He still incarnates among us, in the body of Christ made up of brothers and sisters as organic contributors to each other, according to Paul in 1 Corinthians 12. Indeed, He will always incarnate among us because God the Trinity wishes to have communion with us forever as part of His eternal family. We are family members in Christ's body. We are designed to serve and support each other in Christlike sacrificial love, in intimate fellowship with one another in our Christian communities, which makes us interdependent in the presence of God as our nurturing Trinity parent.

Society needs shaping within families that model their relationships on the gift-love of Father, Son and Spirit, because they are the prime example of perfect relationship. Of course,

---

[291] 1 Corinthians 15:45.

comparisons break down in our language here, as God's being as Trinity is also deeply mysterious. Human families, at their very best, are limited and conflicted by sin. They are not anywhere near close enough to perfect life to be fully descriptive of the mysterious divine inter-Trinitarian life cycle of Father, Son and Spirit. Notwithstanding these limitations, we may anthropomorphise our understanding of God as Trinity family to the extent that this is how God has revealed His life to us in the economy, as Father, Son and Spirit. God, and we, will share united life together in the eternal kingdom of God, made up of all the multicultural people of God.

The Christian Trinitarian family as a safe environment for forming disciples

Creative people are often perceived to be messy. Artists who produce great masterpieces exhibit that mess, with paint on their clothes and seemingly chaotic workshops, the arena where their masterpieces are created. Families need to be instituted on the principle that messiness is welcomed by God in order for creative growth to occur. Our children show us this. We need to welcome and celebrate their messy experiments as they seek to understand their place in the world that belongs to God. This is a compelling picture of God who is creative, and who loves messiness as part of the creative process that leads to great works by those made in Trinity's image.

Children are not born perfect into our families, fully matured and ready for effective adult life. They are untidy, and make numerous errors compared to our adult mature capabilities. They are born to be shaped so that we might participate in their growth, welcoming disorderliness and rewarding it with further encouragement to explore and make yet more mistakes as they mature and develop. Inevitably, the making of mess and childhood experimental mistakes are celebrated rather than condemned by good parents, who laugh with their children as they encourage them to keep on exploring and experimenting with the stuff of the created cosmos.

What a picture of God we can portray through our communities to those who seek to know us better. By doing this, we model God's heart as a loving, nurturing, creative family.

The new perfect creation that came from Elohim's hands was not without messiness. The Trinity already knew that humankind, made in Their image, would choose not to trust Their family, and thus would make a mess, which would be hard to clear up because humankind came to distrust its Father, Mother and Elder Brother, and sinned against Them. Messiness is fine if our children are open to gentle correction by the parents they trust. Messiness is fine among youth and adults as part of the Christian family if they are open to correction as well. But our first parents, Adam and Eve, set in motion a chain of broken life stories where distrust of God and the distortion of His image through cruel misrepresentations of Him led to some terrible stories of human tragedy throughout history. Today we come from varying degrees of distorted pictures of God. What we need to grasp is that the way God may be said to form our pictures of His nature and behaviours also needs to be understood in what we think it means to be made in His image and likeness, as families that welcome messiness as normal parts of human development into the likeness of Christ. This is where it becomes important to understand our human nature as God made it to function in His likeness and image.

Human development in the Trinity-shaped family

Human growth begins with vulnerable children being shaped by sensitive parents who welcome mistakes, muddles and messes. The family nurtures its offspring to grow by providing a safe environment to explore the world. This implies that a functional family that seeks to form its life by the picture of God as an intimate loving family needs to build its primary values around the concept of serving its children through the gift of grace, which allows them to make mistakes as they grow into Christ's likeness, if they choose to. Such a family will encourage them to experiment and make mistakes, because this is how to become a real person made in the

Trinity's image. Human families can be designed to provide safe environments in which messiness and mistakes can be made. As our children make mistakes, they can learn from them to become more like Christ. Our creative God loves mistakes, as all creatives enjoy mess which leads to elegant pieces of work.

The heavenly-earth-man, Jesus, also had to learn in this manner. In His incarnate development from childhood to adulthood, a shaping process was forged that made Him forever God the child (or eternally begotten Son) as much as Jesus the perfect man. This must surely make us sit up in our seats. He declared to His egocentric disciples that the kingdom of God was most naturally defined by a child.[292] Christ Himself had to be smelted in the furnace of His family life as a child, and in broader Jewish society as a Jew. His identity was partly forged on the anvil of experience. He became shaped also as the only begotten Son in whom the Father declared He had complete pleasure, when He was baptised and anointed by the Spirit at His baptism.[293] However, Jesus must have had deep intimacy with God the Mother (Spirit) during His development in order to be nurtured to become the man He did, in whom the Father took pleasure. Lady Wisdom (the Spirit) remained on Him ever afterwards during His earthly mission, and later She was sent to keep going with that mission in participation with the people of Christ, as the Holy Spirit who continued to form Christ's likeness in them as new kingdom people.[294]

The Jesus of incarnation was a messy baby just like we once were. The Jesus we meet in the gospels got angry,[295] cried,[296] laughed[297] and had compassion.[298] He welcomed His muddled

---

[292] Matthew 18:1-5.
[293] Mark 1:11.
[294] Karkkainen, *Pneumatology*, pp. 13, 81, 143,
[295] Mark 3:5.
[296] John 11:35.
[297] Luke 7:34 – Jesus clearly enjoyed celebrations and He must have laughed in company at such events. Luke 10:21 – Jesus rejoiced, which is a higher sense of happiness than simple laughter but includes that emotion.
[298] Matthew 11:28-30; Luke 7:13; Matthew 15:32; Matthew 9:36.

disciples and sought to shape them, for all of their faults. He received messy children who, far from being the least in the kingdom, were its very definition. Such children (men, women, boys and girls) were the most important in God's family, according to Jesus, as models of the humble heart of God modelled by Jesus Himself.[299] How often we make children the unheard minority in our churches. Children's ministry needs to be raised up to the same level of importance as ministry to adults, in my view. Actually, all ministries need to be equalised by the gospel, if we follow Paul's view of equality of all peoples in Christ.[300]

Conclusion

I suggest the most important picture of God to be portrayed by our families and Christian communities is of the Multicultural Trinity who may be portrayed as Father, Mother (Spirit) and Brother (or Sister). I believe that this picture of God will provide Generations Y and Z and third culture children with a compelling understanding of God as their family and their eternal home. The *missio Trinitatis* is based on this view of God's image in which men, women and children have been made. We can only be fully the body of Christ if we are part of this all-inclusive Trinity family.

---

[299] 2 Corinthians 4:1-5.
[300] Galatians 3:28.

Group/personal exercise

In groups of three (or alone), reflect on the questions below.

1. How could a theology of the Christian missional community shaped by social Trinitarian theology help your church community to rethink the way it operates and sees itself as an extension of God's family?

2. What steps could you take in your community to help people explore new ways of viewing God as a missional Trinity that welcomes contributions from all peoples in its work to serve others in the name of Christ?

Part 4

Actively listening to the missional Spirit of the Trinity

Chapter 9
Disciples who discern God's mission

As we have already discovered, Karl Barth, among others, provided the basic principles of a Trinitarian model of the self-revealing God. Of course, the God of revelation is also deeply traditional in the history of the Christian church. Only a God who is personal can be properly thought of as relationally active. The Father sent the Son to reveal God's love to the world. The Son and the Father sent the Spirit to guide God's people to participate in God's mission. In a small volume that Barth wrote, *God in Action*, he comments on God's self-revelation as God in 'action':

> Knowledge of revelation does not mean an abstract knowledge of a God confronting an abstract man. Rather, it is a concrete knowledge of the God who has sought man and meets him in his concrete situation and finds him there. Revelation is a concrete knowledge of God and man in the event brought about by the initiative of a sovereign God. This is what constitutes the glory of God: where the infinite difference between God and man becomes manifest, there indeed it becomes manifest also that man belongs to God not because he is capable of God, not because he has sought and found him, but because it is God's gracious will to make man His own.[301]

This 'concrete knowledge of God' requires that God continues to reveal Himself to people: not to reveal Himself through the Word and sacraments alone, but also through spiritual experiences where God encounters His people. This provides a practical experience-

---

[301] Barth, *God in Action*, pp. 11-12.

based discernment process for practical theologians to discern the *missio Trinitatis*. It also means that the Christian community is a place where people can meet God in action in each other's life experiences. This means the picture of God practically conveyed through Christian lives and communities is one where Christ can be encountered in the life stories of others. Barth did not emphasise spiritual experiences as part of his theology of the Holy Spirit, as such, but we need to include these, alongside what he speaks of as human confession of what God has revealed to His people through Scripture and the sacraments.

Barth's theology of revelation is that God has proactively revealed Himself in the Scriptures and that the Spirit of Christ helps people interpret them. The confession of God's will is part of an ongoing revelation of God by the very act of its confession by the church. God continues to be active behind and through the words of scriptural revelation by which He has spoken. The words of God are alive and active because the God of revelation is still in action through them.

Scripture contains words of significance which continue to impact people's beliefs and actions. This occurs because of the work of the Spirit. There is a strong

> **Identity based on a view of God's kingdom at work among God's people!**
>
> New Life Christian Centre – Scotland
>
> 'The central objective of New Life Christian Centre is to build a prophetic people of Purpose, Prayer, Power, Praise and Prosperity. This mandate is being fulfilled by teaching, training and activating people in the release of the kingdom of God in a simplistic fashion.
>
> We are a people dedicated to equipping the body of Christ to fulfil the great commission of going into all the world and preaching the gospel of salvation to every creature and baptising them in water and in the Holy Ghost with the evidence of speaking in other tongues and laying hands on the sick so that they recover and driving out demonic activity in peoples lives.'
>
> http://www.newlifeministry.co.uk/vision/

prophetic dimension to the work of the Spirit of Christ, according to biblical scholar Ben Witherington III.[302] The Spirit brings the words of God to life, because God has revealed Himself in human history. God enters human history through the words of prophets, priests and kings, and through Christ and His apostles and His people. These words are full of potency when we read them in the Bible. A proper spiritual theology, which is required for followers to receive guidance from God, takes the Bible as the starting point by which all other types of revelatory experiences are to be critically and reflectively measured. There is good evidence that contemporary Christians are still receiving prophetic guidance when it comes to God revealing His plans to new missional situations.

For example, the God who discloses His plans may be claimed to be still active in His self-revelation in Britain. We can see this in the increase of reported spiritual experiences through comparison of two important surveys. In a Gallup National Survey in 1987, of 985 people who were surveyed about religious experiences, 48% reported having them.[303] A repeat survey was done in 2000, which demonstrated a sizeable increase in the numbers of those who reported religious experiences, with 76% reporting them.[304] Sue Pickering comments on the significance of these findings:

> When we put all of this alongside the growing interest in spirituality which has been noted … we see that, particularly for those who do not have any definite

[302] Ben Witherington III, *Jesus the Seer: The Progress of Prophecy*, Minneapolis: Fortress Press (2014), pp. 246-350.

[303] David Hay, *Religious Experience Today: Studying the Facts*, London: Mowbray (1990), pp. 83-85.

[304] David Hay, 'The Spirituality of the Unchurched,' in Mellor, H. and Yates, T. (eds.), *Mission and Spirituality: Creative Ways of Being Church,'* Sheffield: Cliff College Publishing, (2002), p.23.

religious experience points, the possibilities for dialogue about spiritual experience are exciting.[305]

What Pickering highlights connects well with a social Trinitarian perspective, as it may be argued that potential 'for dialogue about spiritual' experiences fits well with a relational view of God, who wants to communicate meaningfully and personally with people by His Spirit. We have already noted that Peter Holmes provides a vision of the social Trinity that has believers shaped by their dialogue with the Spirit of God. His psycho-social theology also allows for an ongoing practical appreciation of discipleship formation in the body of Christ.

Persons are formed in an ongoing process of transformation in dialogue with God. If Holmes is right to encourage us to help people dialogue with the God who speaks, then part of our initial conversations with those who have religious experiences needs to provide some training for them about how to hear God's voice. Those wishing to engage in a proper approach to discipleship formation should seriously consider that the living Christ still wants to communicate with His people. The portrayal of God that has a Christian community hearing His voice is one where believers will be confident that God is alive. Missional practical theology informed by *missio Trinitatis* theology requires that God is alive and actively revealing His actions, plans and purposes to His people. Practical theologians take this conviction to be the fundamental methodological ethos that underpins ethnographic research they do among communities where there is a need to discern the *missio Dei*. A Christian community's words and actions will be a living narrative about the God who loves them and blesses others through them as part of the practical theology lived out by God's people in general.

---

[305] Sue Pickering, *Spiritual Direction: A Practical Introduction*, Norwich: Canterbury Press (2011), pp. 67-68.

Effective spiritual practices

It is important to consider what sorts of spiritual disciplines need to be used to shape us to dialogue with God. First of all, we need to know how to enable people to converse with God. Secondly, how can we ensure that we protect each other from self-delusion? Thirdly, how does a theology of God's self-revelation help a Christian community to develop deeper intimacy with God?

These three questions are often addressed by discussion of spiritual disciplines. The term 'spiritual director' is applied to a person who has the role of helping someone safely explore spiritual disciplines. For those who use this language, the spiritual director needs to have had a number of years of experience in exercising some spiritual disciplines in a healthy, balanced manner in his or her own life in which they have also been accountable to another. The rationale is that those who use the disciplines well are better placed to enable others to experiment with them in a safe manner.

The word 'director' implies that power is one-directional in a relationship of this type. In other words, there is one who directs the other to the essential matters to focus on, and the one who receives direction. In the wrong hands, the power imbalance could lead to abuse of a less experienced, more vulnerable other. Moreover, it does not fit well with a view of social Trinity, where people share their spiritual journeys together equally.

I believe a less formal approach is better. It might take the form of three or four people who agree to commune together by sharing their spiritual journeys. They can learn from each other as they help each other reflect on the strengths, weaknesses, opportunities and threats that they identify together in their spiritual practices. Small accountability groups are a great way to bring balance into the spiritual lives of the people who share them. We may call these informal groups 'soul-friend groups'.

The Celtic Christian writer Ray Simpson offers an important contribution regarding how a soul friend may be defined with regard to mentoring.[306] Soul friends are those who go on a journey alongside people, helping them to grow in intimacy and friendship with the Lord. They necessarily arise out of a Trinity-shaped conviviality. The social Trinity is most certainly a convivial metaphor for a relational deity, where persons share life deeply and openly. In like manner, we can model this kind of intimacy with regard to our spiritual growth.

My practical theology of the Trinity-shaped Christian community is based on the convivial work of the Spirit of Christ as She engages in two actions within each of us. Firstly, the Spirit engages in inner transformation of the human soul. This means that people will become increasingly more like Jesus the representative human being as they model their lives on His. Secondly, the Spirit engages in leading followers to participate in the *missio Trinitatis* to reconcile others into God's eternal family.

The posture of listening

Theology of the self-revealing missionary God needs to be based on the conviction that God communicates with people today. According to Matthew's gospel, Christ commissioned His followers to go to all nations to 'make disciples'. We have turned to this passage a number of times in this book because it is foundational to my theology of MT. The disciples were not to be alone in this venture because Christ would be with them (by the Spirit) until the close of the age.[307] John's gospel testifies that Jesus said:

> 'My sheep hear My voice, and I know them, and they follow Me; and I give eternal life to them, and they will never perish; and no one will snatch them out of My hand. My Father, who has given *them* to Me, is greater

---

[306] Ray Simpson, *Soul Friendship: Celtic Insights into Spiritual Mentoring*, London: Hodder & Stoughton (1999), pp. 9-36.
[307] Matthew 28:19-20.

than all; and no one is able to snatch *them* out of the Father's hand. I and the Father are one.'[308]

This passage needs to be read alongside a later promise which Jesus makes in this gospel, when He claims that the Spirit will continue to communicate with His disciples after His ascension.[309] There is a clear practical theology in the New Testament which asserts that it is normal for a person to receive communications from the ascended Christ in heaven, by the Spirit. Christ's sheep are able to 'hear' Christ's 'voice'. Another way of putting this is to say that Christ communicates with us on an interior psychological level, as Holmes claims. It is the responsibility of the believer to listen to the inner voice of the Spirit and to act upon it. John reminds Christ's followers that just as Jesus had a personal relationship with His disciples, so will the Spirit continue this relationship with them:

> 'I will ask the Father, and He will give you another Helper, that He may be with you forever; *that is* the Spirit of truth, whom the world cannot receive, because it does not see Him or know Him, *but* you know Him because He abides with you and will be in you.'[310]

The word 'helper' is translated from the Greek *parakletos*, which most commonly means, 'one called to our side to help us and advise us'. The theology of John provides a remarkable charismatic case example which helps us to understand how the Spirit of Christ will behave in relationship to believers. Just as Jesus personally communicated with His disciples while He was physically present on earth, so He still communicates in personal terms today, through a kind of inner dialogue with His Spirit. Listening to the God who speaks is a vital part of the spiritual discernment process,[311]

---

308 John 10:27-30, NASB.
309 John 16:12-16.
310 John 14:16-17, NASB.
311 Simon Reed, *Creating Community*, pp. 82-85.

necessary for those who participate in the Trinity's work, to reconcile people into God's MT family.

In my training as a pastoral counsellor, the posture of careful listening was emphasised time and again. Numerous exercises in active listening skills enabled me to help clients explore their thoughts and feelings. Indeed, it is vital to take time to listen to God as much as to people. At the heart of all counselling is the simple practice of active listening. There is a simple formula for active listening, which focuses on repeating back what the counsellor has heard the person say, with a special focus on what it seems they feel. I have found the habit of listening carefully to discover others' thoughts and feelings very useful in my Christian ministry as I have sought to help people overcome obstacles they face. It has also proved helpful to intentionally pay attention to what God communicates to me during quiet times of intentionally listening to Him.

During these quiet times I seek to see, feel and hear what intuitively and spontaneously comes to my mind. It has led to some remarkable insights into myself, and my ministry. I believe God's Spirit brings spontaneous revelations into my mind, which have the uncanny ability to help me overcome personal obstacles in my life. Many people speak of this kind of inner listening as taking time to listen to the 'still, small voice of God', as the prophet Elijah was said to have done after fleeing into the wilderness from Jezebel.[312] There is a simple process which I use to dialogue with God that finds resonances with other forms of Christian meditation and attentiveness.

Listening as four steps

There are four steps in the approach I find works best for me: stillness, attentiveness, spontaneity and reflection. First of all, I intentionally mark out a time in the day or week when I have space to relax and clear my mind of distractions. These distractions may

---

[312] 1 Kings 19:13.

be my to-do list, feelings of inner turmoil, hurt caused by others, excitement over a new project, etc. I use simple deep breathing techniques, accompanied by relaxation exercises, to still my busy mind to a point of peaceful non-engagement with the things of daily life. I also tend to pray for the peace of God to enter my heart, as I become more centred and relaxed during these times.

Once I feel at peace, I then focus on being attentive to random thoughts, feelings, pictures and ideas that flash through my mind. I do not try to capture any of these immediately, but simply trust that what God wants to communicate to me will capture my attention. Much of this book came into being in this way. What often happens is that a theme will become clear in the mixture of these spontaneous intuitions. When they start to appear, I either draw what I see in my journal or keep visualising what appears as pictures in my mind's eye, keeping them at the centre of my attention. I do not try to analyse what comes to me until later.

At other times I entrust everything to memory as things come to me while I am driving, relaxing or falling asleep. This leads me to respond to what is coming to mind, as a kind of dialogue between me and God. Again, I do not try to analyse what comes to mind, but I seek to ask questions if I am not sure what I am seeing or hearing. I find that answers often come as pictures, feelings, ideas or as a reply in a sentence or two.

It helps me sometimes to journal my conversations with God, as this can help me to go with the spontaneous flow of what comes to me. It keeps me from analysing what comes, but rather helps me to stay focused on the spontaneous intuitions.

I normally finish these times with prayers of thanks, asking God to help me reflect on what has come to me as the day or week goes on, so that I may rightly interpret what He may have communicated if it is not simply my imagination working overtime. If I want to reflect later on what has been meaningful, I can go back to my journal and remind myself of the content of particular experiences. I think it is always useful to record what has been revealed if it is especially meaningful, so that we can return to the insights later.

Active listening as *lectio divina*

Lectio divina means 'divine reading'. Those who use this approach effectively might use it to reflect on passages or verses of Scripture that have captured their attention. They may equally carefully consider other things, such as dreams, visions or meaningful life events that have struck them as significant.

Lectio divina helps us to focus our attention on key moments. It follows a simple, loosely held structure that guides us as we reflect on the things that captivate our attention. There are four movements in the process of using *lectio divina*: *lectio*, *meditatio*, *oratio* and *contemplatio*. I find the work of Sue Pickering to be a useful resource to help understand *lectio divina*. I will use pertinent ideas she provides as I highlight the value of this approach.

First of all, we begin with *lectio*, which is described by Pickering as:

> 'Reading' the event or contemporary image that has taken our attention, taking time to explore our initial response to the 'key moment'.[313]

In my own practice of *lectio divina*, I find it helpful to prayerfully ask God to help me explore all that it is important for me to recognise about a key moment I wish to focus on. This can take five minutes or longer. Sometimes I read slowly from the Bible and let the words sink deeply into my consciousness. I take note of my initial responses to the passage, and wait until I feel I have spent enough time with them in the forefront of my mind.

Having got to this point, I then move on to *meditatio*. Pickering makes this comment:

> Thinking, reflecting, exploring, making connections, for example with scripture, with what we know of God through our experience ... with our own situations ... We

---

[313] Pickering, *Spiritual Direction*, p. 74.

listen for the inner promptings of the Holy Spirit who knows what we need to be asking ourselves![314]

We need to pay careful attention to what questions are raised, or what insights come, which will lead us naturally into dialogue with God, the third part of the process, known as *oratio*:

'Talking' to God about what we are discovering about God and about ourselves through this event/image/'key moment'; responding to God with our whole selves, our feelings and our imaginations, our bodies and our minds.'[315]

This prayerful dialogue with God's Spirit is a very real part of my own spiritual experience. I find that spontaneous insights come to mind which had not been clearly present prior to my time of meditation. I can remain in *oratio*-prayer like this for minutes, tens of minutes or at times for an hour. Time is not the measure of the quality of this kind of prayer. It is rather the deeper meaning that comes out of taking time to be in the presence of the God of shalom wholeness that matters, as it helps to stabilise my mind. The Hebrew concept of shalom means more than peace: it implies inner healing that leads to wholeness, which can also include a deep abiding sense of inner integration between the self and God.

This leads to the fourth part of the process, known as *contemplatio*:

Resting in the love of God, letting ourselves open to the Love which waits to enfold us, consenting to the work of the Holy Spirit within us.[316]

Engaging in *lectio divina* can be deeply meaningful. If you know anyone who uses this approach, you may have noticed that it has helped them to resolve matters which make up the 'key moments'

---

[314] Pickering, *Spiritual Direction*, p. 74.
[315] Pickering, *Spiritual Direction*, p. 74.
[316] Pickering, *Spiritual Direction*, p. 74.

in their lives. 'Key moments' include having gone through depression, or grief, or having worked hard to get a promotion at work, or yet again wrestling with a doubt. We may feel overwhelmed by a demotion at work; we may have been treated abusively by an employer who has not consulted us about a change to our role. We may be suffering with lustful sexual obsessions. All of these things need to be brought to shalom wholeness, where we consent to the 'work of the Holy Spirit within us', to transform them so that they no longer dominate our lives. In this sense, *lectio divina* is a great spiritual discipline which fits very well with a social Trinitarian view of relationality. It also fits well with the desire of God for friendship with us in all aspects of our lives.

There is a second sense in which *lectio divina* can help us. This has to do with learning how God wants us to participate in mission with His Spirit. We are all Christ's disciples who, according to Holmes, are to be brought to salugenic[317]wholeness through the inner working of the Spirit.[318] Moreover, part of the salugenic discipleship formation process has to do with us understanding what God wants us to do in our work with others. We may be sure that God is already at work in them. We can focus on 'key moments' when we have talked to others about our faith as opportunities where we have participated with God in His ongoing work in their lives. These could be opportunities with work colleagues, or with friends or family members. *Lectio divina* offers an approach to help us understand how God wants us to proceed, as we move forward with new opportunities to join Him in His mission with faith-seeking people with whom we have friendships.

We can seek to disciple others by taking them through a *lectio divina* process. My view of the formation of new disciples is that each of us, not just professional clergy, can help others to come to know God better, simply by sharing with them the things that have

---

[317] A term used in psychology and therapy meaning the means by which someone becomes whole. The term relates to healing which leads to wholeness.

[318] Holmes, *Trinity in Human Community*, p. 50.

helped us in our own journey with God. A key concern of a practical *missio Trinitatis* theology is the formation of disciples who can dialogue with the missionary God's Spirit. *Lectio divina* provides a wonderful tool for anyone who wants to focus their spiritual energy on a relationship with God. If we help new followers of Christ to dialogue with the Spirit of Jesus for themselves, we connect them to the ever-present Jesus, who once dialogued with His disciples as He walked the dusty roads of Galilee, through the hills of Judea and among the streets of Jerusalem.

The God of action continues to reveal Himself to those who make space and time for Him in their busy schedules. We follow a God who guides us, and sends us, to participate in His mission to reconcile peoples of the world to Godself. Most importantly, practices like *lectio divina* need to become part of the way we intentionally fellowship together as Christians. *Lectio divina* is not a tool to be used as a solitary device, simply for a spiritual 'fix' for ourselves. If we use it in the context of a view of God, as persons co-existing in community, then even our own individual engagement with God through it will be for us to participate in the life and love of Father, Son and Holy

Identity based on persons who are valued by God for their diverse contributions to the Christian community!

Fresh Expressions – UK

'Because there is no standard model of fresh expression of church. They cannot and should not be cloned! Rather there is a process, which is normally followed, when they are established. It begins with listening – to God and to the community or network you are trying to reach. It is more about discernment than strategic planning: Looking for the Holy Spirit's opportunities, and obeying his call. Out of the listening – which may take some time – comes service: a way of serving the people you are trying to reach. Christians who want to share good news need first to be good news, to show genuine concern for others. This is the start of "incarnational mission".'

https://www.freshexpressions.org.uk/about/introduction

Spirit. Even more so, when groups of people use it to fellowship with God and each other, it can lead to deep group bonding because the God of community is able to help us become closer, since His Spirit brings unity among His people. Active love is love where people become closer to God together in a community, rather than simply on their own. This is the subversive narrative of a social theology of *missio Trinitatis*. MT theology also calls us to share deeper spiritual life with other Christian communities.

Listening to our multicultural communities

In this section, we will first of all focus on listening to the people in our churches about what God is saying to them about His mission. Secondly, we will focus on how we might be more attentive to our local unchurched multicultural communities and what God is saying to us through them. The sovereign Spirit of Jesus is ahead of us at work in non-Christian communities. We need to discover the Spirit's voice as She speaks to us from among these communities, to inform our participation with Christ within them. We will need to serve apprenticeships with non-Christian communities, which may be better in touch with the Spirit of Jesus than we are. We need to do this in order to walk more effectively alongside the Spirit, as She transforms these communities into Christ's likeness and we walk alongside Her, following Her footprints in the process of transformation into Christ's likeness that is occurring in another's life.

'Listening out' community vision

Firstly, listening and attentiveness are required to listen effectively to God's voice as it comes through members of our Christian communities. Alan Roxburgh and Fred Romanuk talk of 'listening out' from people, to what God is saying through them.[319] They frame this in what they call their Missional Change Management

---

[319] Alan, J. Roxburgh, and Fred Romanuk, *The Missional Leader: Equipping Your Church to Reach a Changing World,* San Francisco: Jossey Bass (2006), pp. 3-78.

(MCM) process.[320] They contend that in order for a congregation to become more missionally focused on God's mission, leaders need to use the skills of active listening to hear effectively what God is saying to the church through His people.[321] It is vital to listen carefully to what people in the church say about what God is communicating to them.

Their thesis is simple, yet it has profound connections to a social vision of *missio Trinitatis* theology. The authors essentially contend that the church's mission is the people's shared mission with God. It is not just the leader's ideas for mission that count, but it is all the people in the body of Christ through whom God reveals His mission.[322] Simply recognising the revolutionary implications of this view is enough to call for a new type of leadership, where leaders actively listen to their people to enable them to explore, understand and act upon what God wants to do.

It is not building bigger churches that matters, or planting hundreds of new churches, in the first instance. God's mission has always been focused on His people exercising their spiritual gifts to bring Christ to the world and each other, as acts of loving kindness. The church that listens to God together through each other will also provide a picture of the Trinity to those who witness the life of God at work in these communities. God will be observed to be relationally active in the lives of His people, in other words.

Actively listening to others is clearly a very useful approach to adopt if the church wants to equip people to discern God's mission, helping them to listen to God for themselves in the informative atmosphere of the Body of Christ that helps us to weigh up what God is communicating. It will also provide a subversive counterbalance to protect the church from egotistical manipulative leaders. If we give significance to the people of God and to what God is igniting in their imaginations, we will develop a new kind of Trinitarian missional ecclesiology that will be practical, applicable,

---

[320] Roxburgh and Romanuk, *The Missional Leader*, pp. 79-108.
[321] Roxburgh and Romanuk, *The Missional Leader*, pp. 15-36.
[322] Roxburgh and Romanuk, *The Missional Leader*, pp. 61-78.

meaningful and productive. It will rebalance the church to become a community rather than a hierarchy. It will hopefully encourage the people of God to listen to each other and to imagine, alongside the Spirit, what God wants them to participate in as part of Trinity's mission.

I would suggest a simple approach to make this happen. Leaders and the people of the Christian community need to spend much more time getting to know one another on a personal level. They will need to listen intentionally to each other so that they can discern what God is up to in their lives. Over time, this will hopefully help people to identify, and then participate in, what the Spirit is calling them to engage in with God. In other words, God reveals Godself through every one of His people in the body of Christ.

If we want to release the motivating energy of the Spirit of mission in our churches, we need to encourage each other to take seriously that God reveals His plans for mission through the Spirit-inspired creative imaginations of His people. If we want to join together as followers of Christ to see His kingdom of love come on earth as it is in heaven, then, in terms of a spiritual theology of *missio Trinitatis*, fellowship is more important than a beautiful church building. The primary voices through which God guides His people to make missional decisions for action in local communities is by the inspiring presence of His voice, which may be discerned in each of His people.

Attentiveness to communities

Secondly, attentiveness can take the form of observing a local non-Christian community and seeking to listen to people's concerns, challenges and needs. This is really a very basic empirical method. We ask students to take lots of snapshots of the community they want to learn about at my college. This is something you may wish to do. You might want to include photographs of schools, the school gates where parents wait for their children, playgrounds where children go with their parents for fun and games, pubs, bars, community centres, sports clubs, the local shops and the places where young people hang out. Bear in mind that there are important safeguarding issues which Christian churches and other organisations can help you to understand if you do something like this yourself.

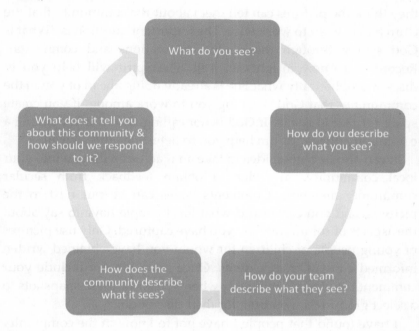

Once the photos have been taken, they can be categorised and put into a scrapbook or uploaded onto a laptop or iPad. The aim is to categorise pictures into thematic groupings, to help describe what a community is like. Captions can be put alongside photos, suggesting something important you have discovered about the community you may want to reach out to. What questions do the pictures make you ask? What strikes you about the character of the community you are looking at? What does this tell you about this community and its needs? Thoughts and observations can be recorded as bullet points next to the pictures.

Once you have described as much about the community from these pictures as you can, show them to members in your church. If you do this, it is important to screen pictures of children because of child protection issues. My practice is normally not to include pictures of local children. You will need to exclude your comments, so they can only see the pictures and form their own reactions. This is so you can listen afresh to what they see happening, and to what they think the pictures can tell them about the community that the church may want to work with. The important question is, 'What is God saying through these new observations and comments?' Record these new insights as well. The Spirit will help you to discern prophetically what She is already doing ahead of you in the communities that God is calling you to work among, if you create space for Her to speak. If God is not calling you to work among a community, the Spirit can help you to determine this as well.

It can also be a good idea to take an iPad out with you into your local community, in order to obtain feedback from secular community members. Comments boxes can be put next to the pictures, and you can record what local people have to say about the aspects of community life you have captured. Only use pictures of young people or children for whom you have obtained written informed consent from parents. Once more, do not include your comments or others' comments when you show these snapshots to a select group who you trust for their discretion.

I have found that people I have got to know in the community are the most helpful in giving feedback. Context matters when you ask for local opinion. I tell people the reason for doing this kind of exercise: that the local church wants to try to understand its community better so it can join in with community life more meaningfully. I give a few examples of benefits that could come from doing this, such as youth clubs, use of church hall facilities for local dance groups, provision of venues for parties, local clubs, etc. It is surprising that people will often respond positively in giving feedback if they have time to do so.

Having gathered all this feedback, bring together all of the comments relevant to each picture in your scrapbook or on your iPad. The next part of the process is to sit down with people in your smaller selected group to ask the broad question, 'What does all of this feedback tell us about this community?' A follow-up question might be, 'What does it seem like the Spirit is revealing to us about God's activity or presence in this community?' As a keen activist, I find it often hard to hold myself back from asking, 'How should we respond to what we have discovered?'

This last question may need to be addressed in the future, where discussion would need to focus on practical missional theology and the use of action–reflection tools. At this juncture, I am simply offering different approaches which can help us to connect with the God who speaks. The earlier diagram provides a simple suggestion for the action–reflection process I have described. Using action–reflection tools like this one can enable your Christian community to engage in God's mission in their communities alongside the Spirit. Being attentive helps to focus our spiritual antennae on what God wants to reveal to us about His mission for a community. It is important to take time and care to develop the skills of focused attention giving and careful listening, so that we may become more centred on learning from God and others about what is really important to God, others and our communities.

Too much missional planning is detached from the incarnational God of ordinary life. Missional leaders can become so caught up in their big plans and strategies to plant new churches that little or no attention is paid to the Spirit of Christ who is active in the unexciting world of the everyday life of secular people. If we are to take Newbigin's theology seriously regarding the Spirit's work among people in society, we will need to set our sights far lower than our fantasies and big plans and projects to build our own little empires. This is because the God of incarnation must, by definition, be incarnationally present alongside ordinary people in urban and suburban contexts.[323] Fresh expressions of new monastic missional communities seek to live among people in cities in their urban contexts, meaningfully serving them.

---

[323] Darren Cronshaw, *Seeking Urban Shalom: Integral Urban Mission in a New Urban World*, Australia: ISUM (2014), pp. 134-136.

Ash Barker offers a critical approach to offer hope to people in the urban context of slums.[324] First and foremost, we should seek to be the presence of Christ to the people among whom we live and work, the people we do business with and care for, alongside the poorest, the downtrodden, the disease-ridden, the outcasts and the prodigals, and all whom we find in our societies' social strata. If God is by definition revealed in a love-united community, then this means God is interested in ordinary communities where people struggle to work out how to live their lives authentically, in the daily rounds of community life. Seeking revelation from God for where He is at work in society will most often be based on His call to work with people in the ordinary rather than in the extraordinary.

Incarnational mission can start with the lowest and least exciting people in our society, as Jesus did. It can include those at the top of society as well, if we use this kind of social analogy. A social theology of *missio Trinitatis* locates the mission of God in the ordinary societies we find ourselves living in. *Missio Trinitatis* is not simply based on being on the move, seeking to plant lots of new churches rapidly, but rather it has to do with God intentionally incarnating by His Spirit in all of the intimate rounds of human life

---

[324] Ash Barker, *Slum Life Rising: How to Enflesh Hope within a New Urban World*, Victoria: UNOH (2012), pp. 233-246.

and daily existence. The picture of God provided by the life and ministry of Jesus occurred in the ordinary and poorest parts of Jewish society. God lives to have relationships and friendships with real people, rather than being the great strategist in the sky who is only interested in making His kingdom into an empire. Empires have a totalitarian ethos, whereas God as the paradigm for community life seeks to walk alongside people, as He and they partake in life together.

Conclusions

This chapter has discussed the God who reveals not simply God's ideas or projects that He wants believers to understand or engage in, but more importantly the social Trinitarian view of God which contends that God reveals Himself personally to humankind. This God of self-revelation needs to be listened to, because first and foremost He is our friend and Father. The Father sent the Son to make His nature of love known to humanity, and thereafter Christ sent His Spirit the Mother to enable His followers to enter into deep communion with the God who speaks. As present-day followers of the Lord Jesus Christ, we need to develop the discipline of attentive listening, not only to the voice of God in Scripture, but also to the voice of the Spirit in our hearts. Modern-day disciples need to be brought to wholeness through the indwelling Christ, as they also engage in MT's mission to disciple others to enter into a similar relationship with God for themselves.

The belief in the social Trinity, a community of persons joined in love as the one God, requires that the persons of God communicate with Their creatures. This is because relationship defines God's nature. From the earliest period of the post-resurrection records of the church, God is said to have actively guided His people by His Spirit.

It is important to give attention to the New Testament records in order to understand some early case examples of how the missionary God interacted with His followers. We have done this already; hence we can move on to the final chapter, which focuses on how we can help our Christian communities be shaped by a social Trinitarian picture of God.

The next question to address is how does a theology of God's self-revelation help a community to spiritually form disciples? Discipleship formation is the number one concern of a practical social *missio Trinitatis* theology.

Part 5

Applied practical missional theology and multicultural missional leaders

Chapter 10
Helping your Christian community shape its picture of God

This chapter focuses on the key question, 'How can leaders help their Christian communities to shape and form their picture/s of God?' I hope we might also ask ourselves the question, 'How can we help our communities shape their picture of God with reference to God as MT?' Of course, MT theology is an ideological vision of what the eternal kingdom will finally and perfectly become. I do not intend to do an in-depth analysis of how such a goal can be achieved. What I write is meant to be taken as suggestive of what a process that answers these questions might need to include.

Generally speaking, practical theologians ask questions about the kinds of methods that might help the communities they write for, to bring about new understandings or to initiate changes of the views of their peoples. I would suggest a broad method, which consists of two components. Firstly, I believe it is important to engage people in our communities in conversations about their pictures of God. Secondly, I think it is useful to adopt a dialectical approach that helps members of the community to learn about varying pictures of God that are held by different communities. Comparing differences and similarities may help them to see God in new ways. The reason for grounding dialectical comparisons between communities on real examples is because people learn best by seeing and experiencing for themselves.

In the 11 following sections, I offer ideas for how your Christian community could be helped to shape and further form its picture of God as it is lived out in your group.

1. Discover the founding story of your Christian community

Counsellors and consultants often seek to help people explore and understand the story that led them to see themselves as they do now. For example, what was it that initially brought a couple together whose relationship is now under threat? What attracted them to each other? The counsellor might encourage them to relate the story of their early romance. By doing this it is possible to help the couple remember what brought them together, to reform their identity together. It is often the case that the couple will describe what they liked in the other. In other words, their initial passion for each other came about because of the characteristics each found attractive in the other's story and appearance.

This is also true of how a Christian church may have come to be planted. Those who have belonged to that church for some time will probably remember the story and the passion of those who planted it. What was that passion based on? What did they sense about God that convinced them that it was God's will for the church to be planted? By helping our community to connect with its roots, we can help them become aware of the passionate claims of their founding story, and how it may still motivate them to gather together as a church in the present context. Attraction is the vital aspect of engaging in this reflective approach, as people were, and may still be, attracted to the picture of God which is reflected in their founding stories.

2. Actively listen to the stories of the people in your community

I take the idea very seriously that we are all organically part of the body of Christ. If, as Paul claims, we have all been given spiritual gifts to build up the body of Christ, it is vital to listen carefully to each other to discover what the living Jesus wants to communicate to His people today through each member of the community. By listening to each other's stories we may come to understand what it is that makes us identify with the Christ we worship together, and

236

to have fellowship with the people with whom we share our faith journeys.

> **Identity based on participating with God in the transformation of a city into God's likeness!**
>
> Holy Trinity Leicester – A mission-shaped church in the heart of Leicester
>
> 'The life of Holy Trinity is shaped by the vision that motivates and inspires us, and by the values we seek to embrace. Let us tell you more about these things…
>
> 'Our vision is that Holy Trinity will be a community that glorifies God by transforming Leicester and beyond. Two key words help us to understand what that transformation involves. The focus of that transformation is that firstly we are transformed by the grace of God shown to us in Jesus and that we grow up in our life and faith into the maturity that Jesus brings to our life. And then we share that grace with others and seek to see that transformation in the lives of people and the city around us.
>
> 'As we follow Jesus in every area of our life we will fulfil his mission of reaching the world with his love. Our dream is to see God's Kingdom come in our lives, and our communities. This is happening as individuals are being transformed by the love and power of God, as families and local communities are being supported by our various practical ministries and initiatives. We want Holy Trinity to be characterised by the love and grace shown us by Jesus – we believe it is this that can bring transformation to our lives and those around us. We believe God brings healing to our lives by his Holy Spirit and by his word and this is an important part of the mission he has called his church to bring to this world.'
>
> http://holytrinityleicester.org/visions-values/

3. What does the locality you meet in, and its environment, say about your community's picture of God?

Take a look around your church building. What do the worship banners convey about your church's picture of God and the identity of its community? What kinds of ministries are going on in the church, and how are they motivated by particular stories about Christ or God in Scripture? What does the overall atmosphere in the church communicate to you and others? How are spaces designed in the church to convey a sense of and focus on God's presence?

You could, of course, look at much more. You might wish to put together a short questionnaire for members and visitors which asks them to share their impressions of how God is pictured by the environment of your place and the use of its spaces.

4. What voluntary ministries are the people engaged in outside the church, or within it?

This is rather a church-centred question, expressed in traditional 'churchy' language. It may be better to ask, 'What ministries do people consider they have in their workplaces, neighbourhoods,[325] clubs, pubs, schools, families and friendship groups?' What picture of God do they have in their mind's eye when they seek to serve others? I believe that for the gospel to impact secular Western society, it requires that we encourage people to see themselves as disciples who model their lives on that of Jesus Christ, who ministered to people at all levels of life. So, for example, what picture of Christ might medical doctors in your church have which enables them to be missional in their work? What picture of Christ do politicians have, etc.?

5. How do outsiders to your community see God reflected in it?

You may ask, 'How can we ask outsiders, who may not have a Christian faith, to talk about a God they do not believe in?' I would say people will respond to reasonable questions which are thoughtfully framed to capture their interest. Try to put together

---

[325] Alan J. Roxburgh, *Missional: Joining God in the Neighborhood*, Grand Rapids: Baker Books (2011), pp. 65-74.

some short questionnaires which can be conducted with willing local community members with whom your community is on friendly terms. Obviously you will use reflections from such questionnaires to communicate with your Christian community about outsiders' views of what the God you convey to them is like. This will be a useful conversation piece, as well as a helpful dialectical tool to enable learning, where those outside the group have different views from what your group actually thinks its community identity should be.

6. How do members see Jesus reflected in each other and by their Christian Community?

People are attracted to communities where they can have real friendships with the people who belong to them. This is not to say that they always see themselves as worthy of the communities they belong to, but at times they attend churches so that they can be influenced by others who they aspire to be like. It can be useful to do anonymous questionnaires with members in your Christian community, including regular visitors, in order to discover what they can see of Christ/God in each other. The most important answers will be those where positive and negative pictures are expressed, which motivate or demotivate people to be part of your community. Once again, you can use the learning from these questionnaires to help your community members understand each other better. Anonymity is therefore important, in order to save people from offence, if remarks are personal. It will be important for those who share the results, for discussion among members of the group, to frame them in a way that will not create conflict, but rather will enable group members to reflect maturely on them together.

7. What is God's purpose for your community?

This question can help uncover the deepest convictions of community members, regarding what they believe their community should do and stand for. People put their beliefs into action. Practical missional theologians are very interested in what people claim to be the purpose that motivates them to behave as they do. For example, there may be a strong feeling among some that engagement in community work, such as doing gardening for elderly people, is a vital way of caring for and supporting them. The

> **Identity based on inclusiveness of everyone in the communities life practices!**
>
> Kingsborough Family Church – Uxbridge
>
> One of their core values is: 'Inclusiveness: In an era of equal opportunities for all, Kingsborough upholds their value on inclusiveness. This implies that anyone and everyone is welcome to be part of our activities and services. Our diverse [multicultural] membership from different nations particularly reflects this and ensures everyone feels at home when they are in Kingsborough. We are a British church and our diversity ensures that we learn [about] cultures from other nations from our members, and so we can adequately accommodate your every need to ensure that when you visit, you feel welcome and have a thrilling experience. This will play a very vital part in your next visit to Kingsborough.'
>
> http://www.kingsborough.org.uk/about.php

picture of God that motivates this kind of purposeful activism may be based on the conviction that Jesus has great compassion[326] for those who are weaker or more vulnerable. Once again, a questionnaire, or some loosely structured interviews with people in your church, may reveal some interesting purpose-driven

---

[326] Ash Barker opens our eyes to a new level of compassion which we share with the poorest, and those who are real outcasts. It is important to learn from his insights, Ash Barker, *Risky Compassion*, Birmingham: Urban Life Together Publishing (2014), pp. 95-114.

behaviours, which at least imply a particular picture of God to be at the foundation of actions that arise from them. This can also help people in our communities to become more aware of the picture/s of God that motivate their behaviours.

8. What is your community's vision and mission statement?

Some churches have developed a broad vision statement of what they believe God's purposes are for them. For example, a vision statement might include:

> We believe that our church has been called to transform our local community to become a peaceful place, where people can be safe to walk at night on the streets without fear of violence.

The vision may seem unattainable, if, for example, the present community has a high level of muggings, gang crime and drug addiction. It may take a long time before the vision of urban peace can be realised. However, the vision statement captures what your Christian group feels God is calling them to do. What is (are) the picture (or pictures) of God portrayed in this case? In order to have arrived at this vision statement, there must have been a process of discernment, through which Christ the peacemaker may have been the picture that informed the prophetic vision, motivating the group to become peacemakers in their community. Their identities will then be formed and shaped by the picture of Christ the peacemaker.

9. Who are the people joining your community and what attracted them to your community?

Obviously you will not want to jump on the first opportunity to interrogate new members to your community as to why they want to be part of it. However, through friendly conversations in social gatherings, you will find that they will often mention in passing what they like about your group. Make some mental notes of these glimpses. What does what they say reveal about the picture of God portrayed by your church? If a leadership team, particularly, can keep a thumbnail sketch of these kinds of helpful conversations, they can find ways of helping their communities to reflect on the picture of God they are conveying to attract new people to join them.

10. What are the most common things people in your Christian community say which expresses how they identify with their community?

There are often common phrases, and jargon, that people use to describe what they like or do not like about their community. Take time to take note of these sayings, in order to gain an understanding of the pictures of God these statements portray. It can be helpful to reflect these kinds of statements back to people in your community, in order to help them hear themselves afresh. This is a common group dynamics tool that is used in group therapy to help group members become more critically aware of what they say about themselves. Obviously, what we say about ourselves or our community identities actually reinforces our behaviours in what we portray about ourselves to each other. Moreover, jargon and sayings that a group often use to describe itself can also capture the picture/s of God that motivates the community to behave as it does.

11. What do your enemies say about your community?

I expect some readers might say, 'But we don't have enemies.' Or there again you might say, 'Yes, I know Mr X fell out with us, but I have forgiven him.' Or, 'Miss C is seriously out of line with us, because she is living with her boyfriend.' There are all kinds of ways we can think about our enemies. Obviously, we would prefer to have no enemies. However, most Christian communities know people, or local groups, who are actively opposed to what they stand for.

It is important to listen for what our enemies identify about our Christian communities that they do not like. This will speak volumes about whether we are really communicating the love of Christ effectively to those who dislike us. Our communities also need to listen carefully to the pictures that their enemies see conveyed by their members. It could be that there is a lot of uncomfortable truth to be found in what our enemies have to say about the identity of our communities, as seen from their perspectives. What they say may imply that the Spirit is prophetically calling our communities to repent of harsh images of God, which in reality have nothing to do with promoting the gospel of peace and forgiveness to our enemies, because we have written them off and treated them harshly. Christ may wish to reach out through us to reconcile us with our enemies.

Conclusions

These 11 suggestions I have shared may prove to be helpful for leaders of Christian communities to use as a loose framework to help their groups have meaningful conversations about the picture of God that their community portrays to others. Moreover, the dialectical comparisons that people can be helped to make when exposed to pictures of God that are different to their own can help them grow and become more open to allowing their lives to be informed by other helpful pictures of God. This will release them and their communities to more fully reflect Christ to others. Indeed, it is my conviction, as a practical Trinitarian theologian, that we need to challenge our Christian communities to consider the picture of God that forms their identity.

My MT theology is based on the conviction that God is bigger than our one tree, which is one among millions of other trees, in God's kingdom forest. If we are willing to embrace others who are different to ourselves, expressive as they are of a more diverse part of God's people, we can learn to accept those differences as part of what it means to be united to the body of Christ in God's kingdom forest. This will always be challenging for us, as it is much easier to remain safe and secure in our own tree in the forest. I believe God is calling us to unite as a diverse multicultural people of God in partnerships and fellowship, as part of MT's family. However, this cannot be forced, and not everyone is being called to do this, and if they are not, they belong to God and will be included in His eschatological eternal kingdom made up of all tongues, peoples and nations. This is *missio Trinitatis* in action. Trinity in action, as God who sends the peoples of His family to reconcile faith-seekers into His family, portrays an activist picture of God to the mobile missional body of Christ.

Postscript

This volume has set out my thinking on how a picture of God based on *missio Trinitatis* and MT can help our Christian communities transform their identities to make them more contextually meaningful to the West's postmodern, pluralistic and multicultural environment. Possibly in a future volume I will set out my vision of how the identities we construct for our Christian missional communities will provide levers that will help us to bring about change in our secular societies. I will let the sociologist Manuel Castells say what I think is at the heart of the importance of identity theory that will help us transform our communities into the kingdom of God as the Spirit creates them anew to belong there:

> The most dramatic social conflicts we have witnessed ... have been induced by the confrontation between opposing identities. Having detected the construction and assertion of identity as being a fundamental lever of social change, regardless of the content of such change, the theoretical interpretation I proposed in my trilogy on The Transformation Age was anchored on the dynamic contradiction between the Net and the Self as an organizing principle of the new historical landscape. The rise of network society and the growing power of identity are intertwined social processes that jointly define globalization, geopolitics, and social transformation in the early twenty-first century.[327]

It will be important to reflect on how human identity taking its vision of God from my MT theology in the context of 'network society' could be enabled to see social transformation take place on a global scale. This would probably require a future volume, should

---

[327] Castells, *The Power of Identity: The Information Age – Economy, Society, and Culture*, volume 2, Chichester: Wiley-Blackwell (2004), p. xvii.

this be pursued. This is the radical claim Jesus made about the kingdom of God which would gather all nations and kingdoms into God's eternal reign. Network society will be co-opted as an extended metaphor to describe the Trinity as an MT networked kingdom community. The *missio Trinitatis* will need to come in the process of network society's networking complexity in fast interchanges between human communities on a global scale.

Bibliography

Adogame, Afe; Gerloff, Roswith and Hock, Klaus, (eds.), *Christianity in Africa and the African Diaspora: The Appropriation of a Scattered Heritage*, London: Continuum International Publishing Group (2008).

Allison, Dale C., *Constructing Jesus: Memory, Imagination and History*, Grand Rapids: SPCK (2010).

Andrews, Dave, *A Divine Society: The Trinity, Community and Society*, Eugene: Wipf & Stock (2008).

Aune, David E., *The Cultic Setting of Realized Eschatology in Early Christianity*, Leiden: Brill (1972).

Barker, Ash, *Risky Compassion*, Birmingham: Urban Life Together Publishing (2014).

Barker, Ash, *Slum Life Rising: How to Enflesh Hope within a New Urban World*, Victoria: UNOH (2012).

Barth, Karl, *God in Action*, New York: Round Table Press (1963).

Barth, Karl, *Church Dogmatics*, Bromiley, G. W. and Torrance, T. F., (eds.), *The Doctrine of the Word of God*, Vol. 1.1, Peabody: Hendricksen Publishers (2010 edition).

Barth, Karl, *Church Dogmatics*, Bromiley, G. W. and Torrance, T. F., (eds.), *The Doctrine of the Word of God*, Vol. 1.2, Peabody: Hendricksen Publishers (2010 edition).

Bartholomew, Craig G. and Goheen, Michael W., *The Drama of Scripture Finding our Place in the Biblical Story*, London: SPCK (2014).

Bauckham, Richard, *Jesus and the Eyewitnesses: The Gospels as Eyewitness Testimony*, Cambridge: Eerdmans (2006).

Bevans, Stephen B., *Models of Contextual Theology (Faith and Cultures)*, Maryknoll: Orbis Books (2002).

Bevans, Stephen B. and Schroeder, Roger P., *Prophetic Dialogue: Reflections on Christian Mission Today*, Maryknoll: Orbis Books (2011).

Bevans, Stephen B. and Tahaafe-Williams, Katalina, *Contextual Theology for the Twenty-First Century*, Eugene: Pickwick Publications (2011).

Boff, Leonardo, *Cry of the Earth, Cry of the Poor*, Maryknoll: Orbis Books (1997).

Bosch, David, *Transforming Mission: Paradigm Shifts in Theology of Mission*, Maryknoll: Orbis Books (2000).

Bruteau, Beatrice, *God's Ecstasy: The Creation of a Self-Creating World*, New York: The Crossroad Publishing Company (1997).

Cameron, Charles M., John Hick's Religious World', *Evangel* 15.1 (Spring 1997).

Cassidy, Laurie and O'Connell, Maureen, H., (Eds.), *She Who Imagines: Feminist Theological Aesthetics*, Collegeville: Liturgical Press (2012).

Castells, Manuel, *The Power of Identity: The Information Age – Economy, Society, and Culture*, volume 2, Chichester: Wiley-Blackwell (2004).

Collicutt, Joanna, *The Psychology of Christian Character Formation*, Norwich: SCM Press (2015).

Cronshaw, Darren, *Seeking Urban Shalom: Integral Urban Mission in a New Urban World*, Australia: ISUM (2014).

Davies, Brian, *Philosophy of Religion: A Guide and Anthology*, Oxford: Oxford University Press (2000).

Day, John, *From Creation to Babel: Studies in Genesis 1–11*, London: Bloomsbury T & T Clark (2015).

DeConick, April, D., *Voices of the Mystics: Early Christian Discourse in the Gospels of John and Thomas and Other Ancient Christian Literature*, Sheffield: Sheffield Academic Press (2001).

Dorr, Donal, *Spirituality of Leadership: Inspiration, Empowerment, Intuition and Discernment*, Dublin: The Columba Press (2006).

Drane, John, *Do Christians Know How to be Spiritual? The Rise of New Spirituality and the Mission of the Church*, London: Darton Longman and Todd (2005).

Dunn, James D., *Jesus and the Spirit*, London: SCM Press (1970).

Fiddes, Paul S. *Participating in God: A Pastoral Doctrine of the Trinity*, Louisville: Westminster John Knox Press (2000).

Flett, John G., *The Witness of God: The Trinity, Missio Dei, Karl Barth, and the Nature of Christian Community*, Grand Rapids: Eerdmans (2010).

Foster, Richard, *Celebration of Disciplines: The Path to Spiritual Growth*, London: Hodder & Stoughton (1989).

Frost, Michael and Hirsch, Alan, *The Shaping of Things to Come: Innovation and Mission For the 21st Century Church*, Australia: Baker Publishing Group (2013).

Gerkin, Charles V., *The Living Human Document: Revisioning Pastoral Counseling in a Hermeneutical Mode*, Abingdon Press (1984).

Grenz, Stanley, J., *Rediscovering The Triune God: The Trinity in Contemporary Theology*, Minneapolis: Fortress Press (2004).

Hanciles, Jehu, J., *Beyond Christendom: Globalization, African Migration and the Transformation of the West*, Maryknoll: Orbis Books (2008).

Andrew, R. Hardy, 'Spiritual and Missional Philosophical Theology', (2012), Doctoral Thesis, Available at: https://www.academia.edu/2416319/Mission_and_Spirituality.

Hardy, Andrew R. and Yarnell, Dan, *Forming Multicultural Partnerships: Church Planting in a Divided Society*, Watford: Instant Apostle (2015).

Harvey, Lincoln, *A Brief Theology of Sport*, London: SCM Press (2014).

Hay, David, *Religious Experience Today: Studying the Facts*, London: Mowbray (1990).

Holmes, Peter R., *Trinity in Human Community: Exploring Congregational Life in the Image of the Social Trinity*, Milton Keynes: Paternoster (2006).

Holmes, Peter R. and Williams, Susan B., *Becoming More Like Christ: Introducing a Biblical-contemporary Journey*, London: Paternoster (2007).

Holmes, Peter R., *Becoming More Human: Exploring the Interface of Spirituality, Discipleship and Therapeutic Faith Community*, Milton Keynes: Paternoster (2005).

Hunter, A. M., *The Work and Words of Jesus*, London: SCM Press (1973).

Hurtado, Larry W., *Lord Jesus Christ: Devotion to Jesus in Earliest Christianity*, Grand Rapids: Eerdmans (2005).

Karkkainen, Veli-Matti, *An Introduction to Ecclesiology*, Downers Grove: IVP (2002).

Karkkainen, Veli-Matti, *Pneumatology: The Holy Spirit in Ecumenical, International, and Contextual Perspective*, Grand Rapids: Baker Academic (2002).

Karkkainen, Veli-Matti, *Trinity and Religious Pluralism: The Doctrine of the Trinity in Christian Theology of Religions*, Aldershot: Ashgate (2004).

Karkkainen, Veli-Matti, *The Trinity: Global Perspectives*, Louisville: Westminster John Knox Press (2007).

Kimball, Dan, *The Emerging Church: Vintage Christianity for New Generations*, Grand Rapids: Zondervan (2003).

Kim, Kirsteen, *Joining in with the Spirit: Connecting World Church and Local Mission*, London: Epworth (2010).

Kittel, Gerhard, (ed.), *Theological Dictionary of the New Testament*, Vol. 1, Grand Rapids: Eerdmans (1979).

Ledwith, Margaret, *Community Development: A Critical Approach*, Bristol: BASW (2011).

Lewis, C. S., *The Magician's Nephew*, London: Harper Collins Children's Books (1998).

Longenecker, Richard, N., *Biblical Exegesis in the Apostolic Period*, Grand Rapids: Eerdmans (1999).

Martin, Dale, B., *New Testament History and Literature*, New Haven: Yale University Press (2012).

McClintock Fulkerson, Mary and Briggs, Sheila, *The Oxford Handbook of Feminist Theology*, Oxford: Oxford University Press (2013).

Mellor, Howard, and Yates, Timothy (eds.), *Mission and Spirituality: Creative Ways of Being Church*, Sheffield: Cliff College Publishing (2002).

Moltmann, Jurgen, *The Crucified God*, London: SCM Press (2008).

Moltmann, Jurgen, *The Trinity and the Kingdom of God*, London: SCM Press (1981).

Moynagh, Michael, *Being Church, Doing Life: Creating Gospel Communities Where Life Happens*, Oxford: Monarch Books (2014).

Murray, Stuart, *The Naked Anabaptist: The Bare Essentials of a Radical Faith*, Milton Keynes: Paternoster (2011).

Murray Williams, Stuart and Sian, *Multi-Voiced Church*, Milton Keynes: Paternoster (2011).

Newbigin, Lesslie, *The Gospel in a Pluralist society*, Grand Rapids: Eerdmans (1989).

Newbigin, Lesslie, *The Open Secret: An Introduction to the Theology of Mission*, London: SPCK (1996).

Neyrey, Jerome, H. (ed.), *The Social World of Luke–Acts: Models for Interpretation*, Peabody: Hendricksen Publishers (2005).

Pickering, Sue, *Spiritual Direction: A Practical Introduction*, Norwich: Canterbury Press (2011).

Oxbrow, Rev Canon Mark, *Trinity and Mission – a review of sources* Pub: Mission Round Table (Occasional Bulletin of OMF Research) Sept 2012 Vol 7 No. 2.

Rahner, Karl, *The Trinity*, Translated by Donceel Joseph, New York: Herder and Herder (1970).

Reed, Simon, *Creating Community: Ancient Ways for Modern Churches*, Abingdon: The Bible Reading Fellowship (2013).

Roxburgh, Alan J., *Missional: Joining God in the Neighborhood*, Grand Rapids: Baker Books (2011).

Roxburgh, Alan J., *The Sky is Falling!?! Leaders Lost in Transition*, Colorado: ACI Publishing (2005).

Roxburgh, Alan J. and Romanuk, Fred, *The Missional Leader: Equipping Your Church to Reach a Changing World*, San Francisco: Jossey Bass (2006).

Savage, Sara; Collins-Mayo, Sylvia and Mayo, Bob, *Making Sense of Generation Y: The World View of 15- 25-year-olds*, London: Church House Publishing (2011).

Schnabel, Eckhard J., *Early Christian Mission: Jesus and the Twelve*, Vol. 1, Downers Grove: IVP (2004).

Simpson, Ray, *Soul Friendship: Celtic Insights into Spiritual Mentoring*, London: Hodder & Stoughton (1999).

Sine, Tom, *The New Conspirators: Creating the Future One Mustard Seed at a Time*, Downers Grove: IVP Books (2008).

Spencer, F. Scott, *Journeying through Acts: A Literary–Cultural Reading*, Peabody: Hendricksen Publishers (2004).

Spencer, Linbert, *Building Multi-ethnic Church*, London: SPCK (2007).

Stanton, Graham, *The Gospels of Jesus*, Oxford: Oxford University Press (2002).

Tajfel, H. and Turner, J. C., 'An integrative theory of intergroup conflict', in Austin, W. G. and Worchel, S., (eds.), *The Social Psychology of Intergroup Relations*, Monterey: Brooks Cole (1979).

Tennent, Timothy, C., *Invitation to World Missions: A Trinitarian Missiology for the Twenty-first Century*, Grand Rapids: Kregel Publications (2010).

Thompson, Judith, *Theological Reflection*, London: SCM Press (2012).

Vreeland, Derek, *Shape Shifters: How God Changes the Human Heart: A Trinitarian Vision of Spiritual Transformation*, Tulsa: Word & Spirit Press (2008).

Watters, Ethan, *Urban Tribes: Are Friends the New Family?* London: Bloomsbury (2004).

White, L. Michael, *Scripting Jesus: The Gospels in Rewrite*, New York: HarperOne (2011).

Witherington III, Ben, *Jesus the Seer: The Progress of Prophecy*, Minneapolis: Fortress Press (2014).

Wright, Christopher, J. H., *The Mission of God's People: A Biblical Theology of the Church's Mission*, Grand Rapids: Zondervan (2010).

Wright, N. T., *Paul: Fresh Perspectives*, London: SPCK (2005).

Wright, N. T., *How God became King*, London: SPCK (2012).

Wright, N. T., *The New Testament and the People of God*, London: SPCK (1992).

Zizioulas, John D., *Being as Communion*, London: Darton Longman and Todd (2013).

Zizioulas, John D., *The Eucharistic Communion and the World*, London: T & T Clark (2011).

Articles and websites

Christ-church, Deal. Available at http://ccd.xpha.net/

Formission College. Available at http://formission.org.uk/

Christians in Sport. Available at
http://www.christiansinsport.org.uk/

Daily Telegraph, 'Gen Z, Gen Y, baby boomers – a guide to the
generations', July 2014. Available at
http://www.telegraph.co.uk/news/features/11002767/Gen-Z-
Gen-Y-baby-boomers-a-guide-to-the-generations.html

Fresh Expressions, 'What is a fresh expression?' Available at
http://www.freshexpressions.org.uk/about/whatis

Stanford Encyclopedia of Philosophy, 'Colonialism', May 2006.
Available at http://plato.stanford.edu/entries/colonialism/